Street by Str

C000173759

SUSSEX

PLUS HASLEMERE

Enlarged Areas Bognor Regis, Brighton, Chichester, Crawley, Eastbourne, Hastings, Horsham, Lewes, Newhaven, Worthing

1st edition May 2001

© Automobile Association Developments Limited 2001

This product includes map data licensed from Ordnance Survey® with the permission of the Controller of Her Majesty's Stationery Office. © Crown copyright 2000. All rights reserved. Licence No: 399221.

Published by AA Publishing (a trading name of Automobile Association Developments Limited, whose registered office is Norfolk House, Priestley Road, Basingstoke, Hampshire, RG24 9NY. Registered number 1878835).

Mapping produced by the Cartographic Department of The Automobile Association.

A CIP Catalogue record for this book is available from the British Library.

Printed by in Italy by Printer Trento srl

The contents of this atlas are believed to be correct at the time of the latest revision. However, the publishers cannot be held responsible for loss occasioned to any person acting or refraining from action as a result of any material in this atlas, nor for any errors, omissions or changes in such material. The publishers would welcome information to correct any errors or omissions and to keep this atlas up to date. Please write to Publishing, The Automobile Association, Fanum House, Basing View, Basingstoke, Hampshire, RG21 4EA.

Ref: MD024

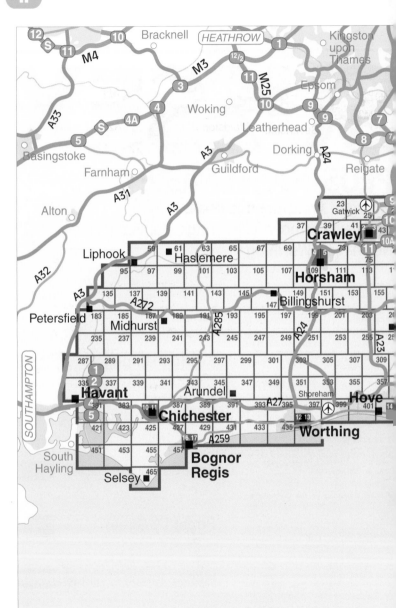

ii

Enlarged scale pages   1:17,500   3.6 inches to 1 mile

| 0 | 1/2 | miles | 1 |
| 0 | 1/2 | 1 | kilometres | 1 1/2 |

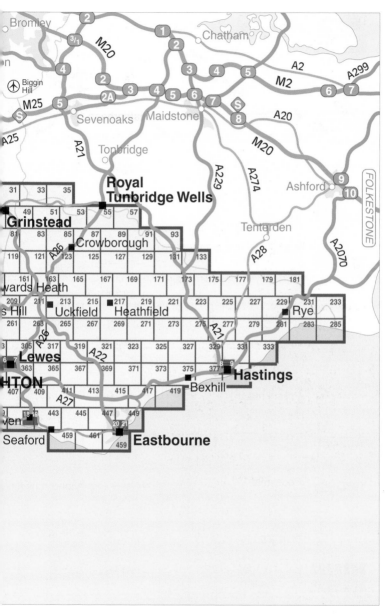

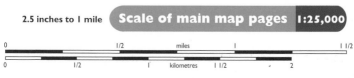

iv

Symbol	Description
Junction 9	Motorway & junction
Services	Motorway service area
	Primary road single/dual carriageway
Services	Primary road service area
	A road single/dual carriageway
	B road single/dual carriageway
	Other road single/dual carriageway
	Restricted road
	Private road
← ←	One way street
	Pedestrian street
---------	Track/footpath
	Road under construction
}- - - -{	Road tunnel
P	Parking

Symbol	Description
P+	Park & Ride
	Bus/coach station
	Railway & main railway station
	Railway & minor railway station
⊖	Underground station
⊖	Light railway & station
+++++++	Preserved private railway
LC	Level crossing
•—•—•	Tramway
---------	Ferry route
....	Airport runway
– · – · – ·	Boundaries-borough/district
ꝟꝟꝟꝟꝟ	Mounds
93	Page continuation 1:25,000
7	Page continuation to enlarged scale 1:17,500

 River/canal lake, pier		♿	Toilet with disabled facilities
Aqueduct lock, weir		🏠	Petrol station
465 ▲ Winter Hill	Peak (with height in metres)	PH	Public house
	Beach	PO	Post Office
	Coniferous woodland	📖	Public library
	Broadleaved woodland	ℹ	Tourist Information Centre
	Mixed woodland	♜	Castle
	Park	🏛	Historic house/building
	Cemetery	Wakehurst Place NT	National Trust property
	Built-up area	🅼	Museum/art gallery
	Featured building	✝	Church/chapel
⊓⊓⊓⊓⊓	City wall	☗	Country park
A&E	Accident & Emergency hospital	🎭	Theatre/performing arts
🚻	Toilet	👥	Cinema

2

Ifield Green

Ifield

Ifield Green

West Green

Gossops Green

Southgate

A3
1 Cotswold Cl
2 Ginhams Rd
3 Pennine Cl
4 Quantock Cl
5 Snell Hatch
Corner Surgery

A5
1 Borrowdale Cl
2 Calderdale Cl
3 Ennerdale Cl

A6
1 Bilberry Cl
2 Bluebell Cl
3 Burbeach Cl
4 Harris Cl
5 Primrose Cl 6 Stonecrop Cl

B1
1 Heron Cl
2 Kestrel Cl

B2
1 Reynolds Pl
2 Spurgeon Cl

B3
1 Church St
2 Lodge Cl
3 Prospect Pl
4 St John's Rd
5 St Peter's Rd

B4
1 Hill Pl

B5
1 Biggin Cl
2 Blackcap Cl
3 Crockham Cl
4 Grisedale Cl
5 Hindhead Cl
6 Patterdale Cl

B6
1 Swaledale Cl

C1
1 Chaffinch Cl
2 Connaught Gdns
3 Martin Cl
4 Short Cl

C2
1 Beech Tree Cl
2 Clappers Ga
3 Marlow Ct

C3
1 High St
2 The Square

C4
1 Station Rd

A1
1 Deerswood Cl

A2

B1
1 Binstead Cl
2 Birdham Cl
3 Colgate Cl
4 Mole Cl

C5
1 Falmer Cl
2 Kithurst Cl
3 Oakhaven
4 Sullington Hl

Leacroft Medical Practice

Crawley College

West Green County First School

Crawley Hosp

Leacroft Medical Practice

A&E

Hollywood Bowl

Virgin Multiplex Cinema

St Georges Ct

Windmill Court

Longmere Rd

A M F Bowling

St Wilfrids RC School

Holy Trinity C of E School

Holmbury Cl

Southgate School

Southgate Middle School

First School

Thomas Bennett Community College

Ifield Primary School

Ifield Community College

Ifield Middle School

CRAWLEY AVENUE

HORSHAM ROAD

BRIGHTON ROAD

A2220

A2219

A23

A24

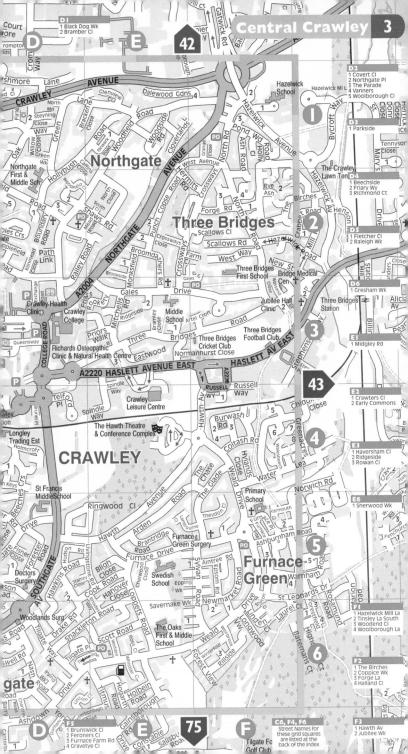

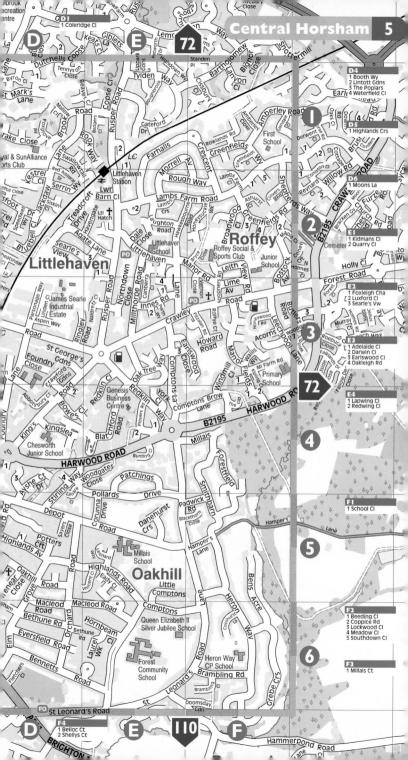

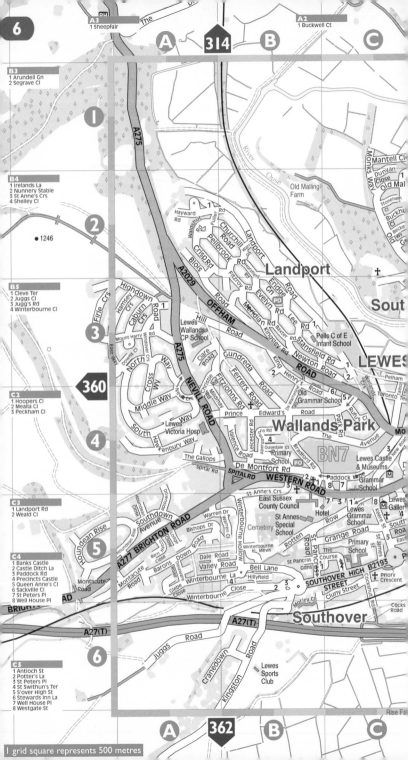

I grid square represents 500 metres

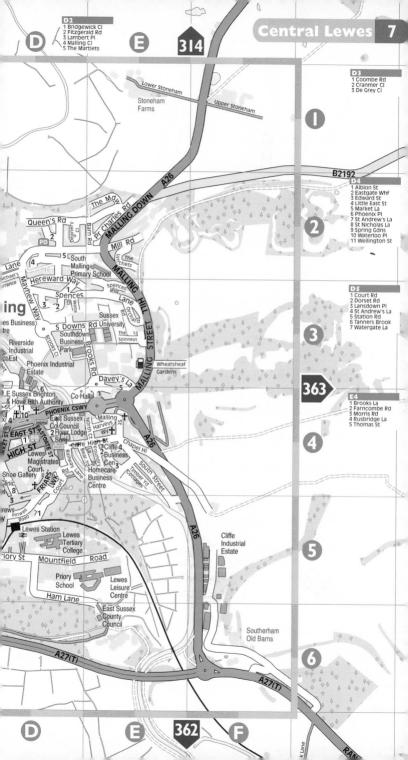

I grid square represents 500 metres

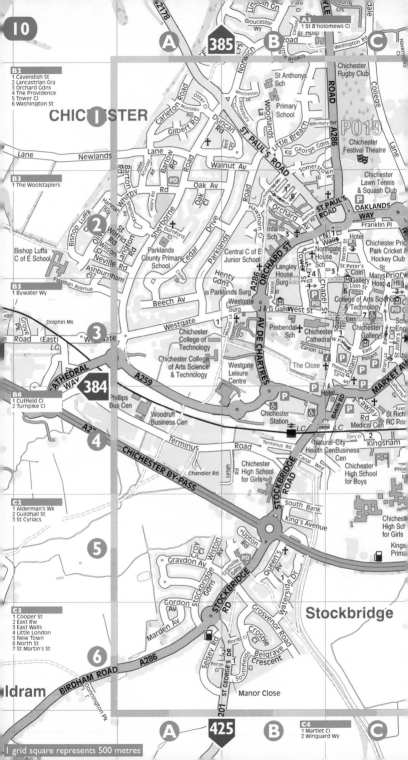

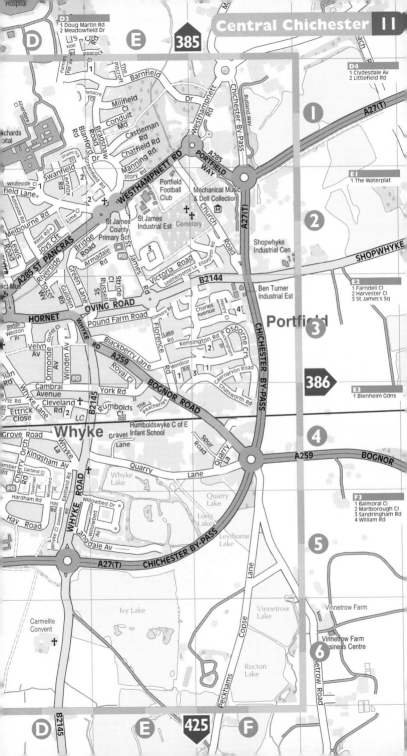

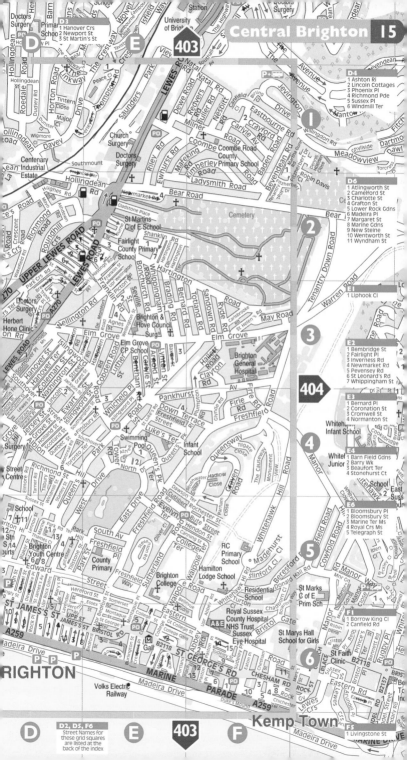

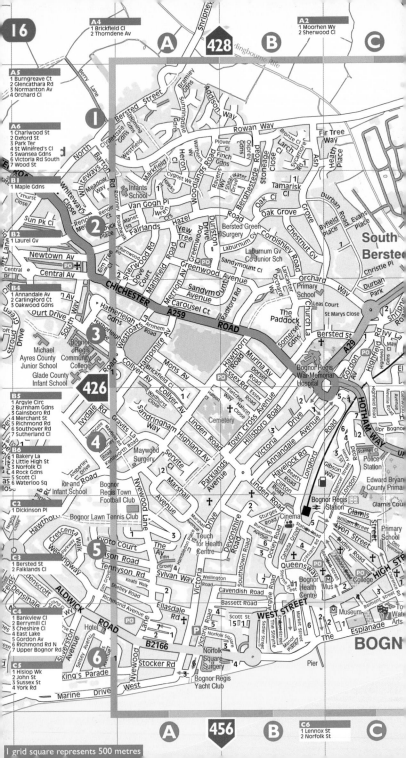

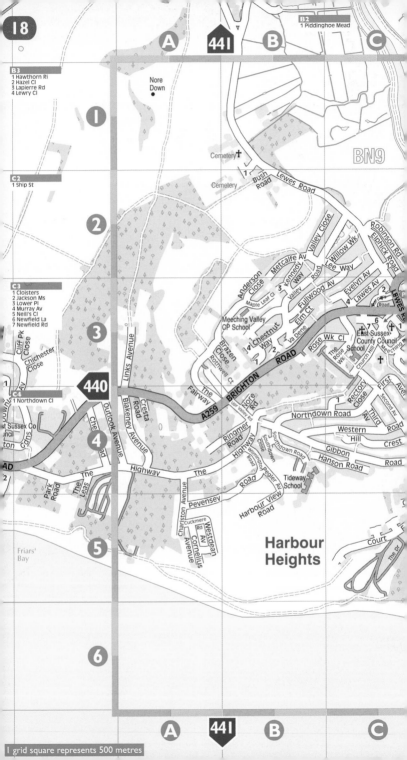

18

○

A **441** B C

B2
1 Piddinghoe Mead

Nore Down

Cemetery †

Cemetery

7 Bush Road

Lewes Road

BN9

Valley Close

Robinson Rd

Fitznick Road

Willow Wk

Lee Way

Metcalfe Av

Anderson Close

Kennedy Way

Valley Road

Fullwood Av

Evelyn Av

Lawes Av

Maple Leaf Cl

LEWES Rd

Meeching Valley CP School

Elm Ct

Va Dene

East Sussex County Council School

Chestnut Way

Rose Wk Cl

The Rose Wk

Meeching

Brazen Close

Rothwell Ct

BRIGHTON ROAD

church hill

Links Avenue

The Fairway

Upr Valley Rd

Nore Rd

Rectory Close

First Avenue

Cliff Pk Close

Chichester Close

440

Cresta

Blakeney Avenue

Outlook Avenue

Chelmer Rd

Northdown Road

Second Av

Western Hill

Third Road

East Sussex Co Council ton

Ringmer Road

Highway

Southdown Close

Southdown Road

Wilmington Close

Pegler Av

Crest

Gibbon

Hanson Road

Road

A259

Park Road

The Leas

Highway

The Road

Charleston Avenue

Pevensey Road

Cuckmere Rd Av

Westdean Av

Cornelius Avenue

Harbour View Road

Tideway School

Harbour Heights

Court

The Dr

Friars' Bay

440

441

A **441** B C

I grid square represents 500 metres

D1
1 Churchdale Pl

Roselands 448

D2
1 Avondale Rd
2 Clarence Rd

Jervis

Prince

1

D3
1 Albion Rd
2 Beltring Ter
3 Chawbrook Rd
4 Havelock Rd
5 Hoad Rd
6 Neville Rd
7 Oxford Rd
8 St George's Rd
9 Sheen Rd
10 Springfield Rd
11 Stanley Rd
12 Willowfield Rd

2

Eastbourne United
Football Club

Guestling Rd

Winifred Lee
Health Centre

D4
1 Burfield Rd
2 Cavendish Pl
3 Colonade Rd
4 Leaf Hall Rd
5 Lion La
6 Marine Rd
7 Qu's Co'ade Gdns
8 St Aubyn's Rd
9 Willowfield Sq

3

Eastbourne
Sovereign
Sailing Club

The
Redoubt

449

D5
1 Burlington Rd
2 Cavendish Pl
3 Elms Rd

4

Seaside
Medical
Centre

Primary
School

Salvation
Army

Hotel

E1
1 Burleigh Pl
2 Roseveare Rd

Hotel

Royal Hippodrome Theatre

Eastbourne
Pier

5

E2
1 Belle Vue Rd
2 Romney St
3 Roselands Cl

stand

6

D   E3
    1 Bayham Rd
    2 Halton Rd   E   462   F
    3 St James Rd
    4 Taddington Rd

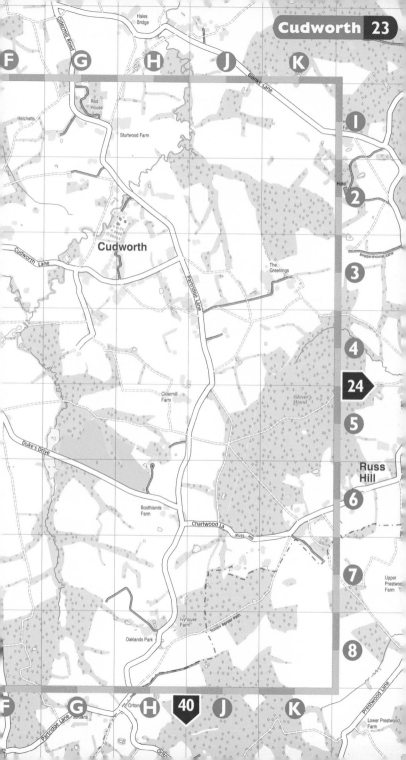

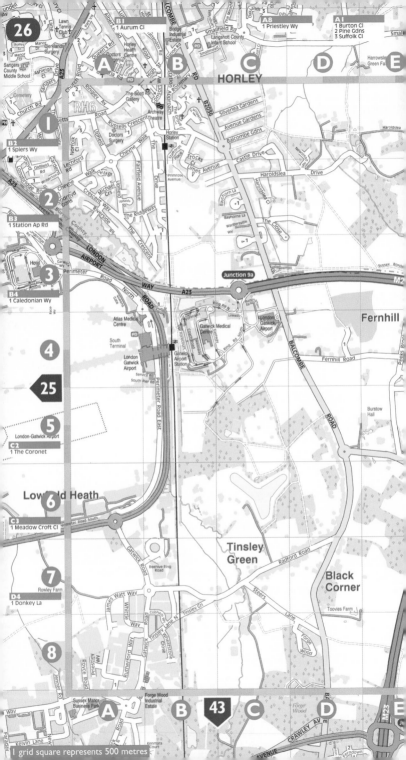

F **G** **H** **J** **K**

1 The Lindens

Perrylands Lane

Smallfield

Bridgeham Grange

Broadbridge

Geary Close

Park Road

Cross Lane

Church Road

Burstow

Rede Hall

Redeham Hall

Rough Beech

Dowlands Farm

Keepers Farm

Green Farm

Shipley Bridge

LANE

ANTLANDS

Newhouse Farm

Courtlands

Shipleybridge Lane

B2037

EFFINGHAM ROAD

B2037

East Hill Lane

Beechfield

Rowland Close

Heatherley

Clay Hall Lane

Copthorne Bank

Roffey's Close

Eiger Way

Oak Close

Westway

Bridgelands

Erica Way

The Copthorne Business Centre

The Meadow

Akehurst Close

Brookhill Close

Bramble Close

Fairway

Copthorne Common

COPTHORNE

A264 COPTHORNE

Francis Gardens

Borers

Arms

Spring Gardens

Borers Business Park

Copthorne Golf Club

Lashmere

Mill Lane

COMMON ROAD

Copthorne Squash Club

Hotel

HORNE WAY

F **G** **H** **J** **K**

28

44

Junction 9

M23

Peeks Brook Lane

1 **2** **3** **4** **5** **6** **7** **8**

Dowlands Lane

Effingham Lane

F8
1 Kindersley Cl

F   G   H   J   K

I

2

3

4

32

5

6

7

8

Ford Manor Road

mansland

Greathed Manor

Hollow Lane

Hill Lane

Hill

dons

Ladycross Farm

Old Lodge Farm

Moors Lane

Sussex Border Path

Upper Stonehurst Farm

Hollow Lane

Lower Stonehurst Farm

Lullenden

Shepherdsgrove Lane

Hoopers Farm

Vanguard Way

Vanguard Way

Moors Lane

Surrey County

Kent County

Wilderwick House

Blockfield Wood

Sussex Border Path

Surrey County
West Sussex County

Gotwick Manor

Vanguard Way

rling Way

Fairlight

Gotwick Farm

Orchards

East Sussex County
West Sussex County

HOLTYE ROAD   A264

Vanguard Way

F   G   H   48   J   K

nheim
Avenue

Shovelstrode Lane

Shovelstrode Manor

Brooklands

grid square represents 500 metres

GS
1 Prior's Wy

Stick Hill

F G H J K

Wilderness Farm

1

Markbeech

PH

Eden Hall (Convent) Falconhurst

Cowden Pound

Gilridge

2

Horshoe Green

Edells

Polefields

Claydene

Pyle Gate Farm

B2026

Cowden Station

3

Wicken

Boggle Lane

The Paddocks

Moat Lane

4

Glover's Hawes

B2026

Saxbys

Leighton Manor Farm

North Street

34

5

Kent County
East Sussex County

Holywych House

Cowden

Chantlers Croad
Church Street
Cowden Mews

Holywych Farm

6

High Street

Sussex House Farm

Hollye House

7

Helhe

Cullinghurst Farm

HARTFIELD ROAD

B2026

8

F G H **50** J K

Edenbridge Road

Chantlers Farm

Tye Farm

EDENBRIDGE RD

HARTFIELD ROAD

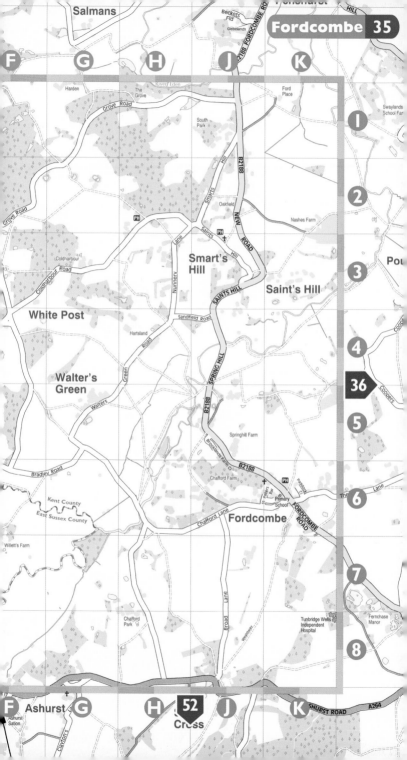

36

A   B   C   D   E

Pond Head Lane

Mayes Green

Lowerhouse Farm

Hotel

1

standon Lane

Horsham Road

2   Horsham Road

Froggetts Lane

Walliswood Farm

Walliswood

PH

Oakfields

3

Somersbury Wood

Oak

4

Smokejack Farm

Hilhouse Farm

5

Horsham Road

Broadstone Farm

Honeywood Lane

Monks Pine

6

Pinkhurst Farm

Stane Rocks Farm

7

Furzen Lane

Honeywood House

Furzen Lane

Ellens

8

Ridge Farm

Horsham Road

A   B   **69**   C   D   E

I grid square represents 500 metres

New Barn Lane
Cathill Lane
Standon Lane
PH
STANE STREET

F
G
H
J
K

I

2

3

Standon Homestead

Leith Vale

Eversheds Farm

Oakwood Mill Farm

Waley's Lane

Waleys

Hale House

4

Oakdale Farm

Sussex

Paynes Green

Weare Street

Sussex Border Path

Sandpits

Ruckmans Lane
Boswells Farm
Place Farm

BOGNOR ROAD

38

A29

North River

Denne Farm

5

Ruckmans Lane

Surrey County
West Sussex County
Sussex Border Path

harmans Farm

6

Northlands
Northlands Business Park

Marches Road
Stone Farm

7
Farm

Mayes Lane

Chatfolds

BOGNOR ROAD

8

harmans Farm

F
G
H
70
J
name Lee
K

Road

F G H 22 J K

Taylors

Lyne House

Cowix Farm

Ridge Farm

Highams

Capel Road

Mudgeridge's Hill

Sussex Border Path

New Barn Farm

Friday Street

Sussex Border Path

Stammerham Business Centre

Sussex Border Path

Rusper

Rusper School

Ashmore

Horsham Road

40

Dial Post Farm

Friday Street

The Nunnery

Great Benhams

Manns Farm

Baldhorns Park

Wimland Road

Horsham Road

Green Lane

Wimland Road

Green Lane

Coombers Farm

Old Holbrook

Hilltop Farm

Wimland Farm

Wimland Hill

F G H 72 J K

I Farm

2 Capel Road

Pollingfold

3

4

5

6

7

8

Sussex Border Path

A   B   23   C   D   E

Oaklands Park

Ivyhouse Farm

Sussex Border Path

1

Chaffold's Farm

Orltons

Jordans

Partridge Lane

2

Rusper Road

Sussex Border Path

Surrey County
West Sussex County

Orltons Lane

Langhurst

The

Capel Rd

3

Highams

Newdigate Road

Sussex Border Path

Chowles

Langhurst Lane

4

Rusper

School

PO

East Street

Burnt House Lane

Rusper Road

39

Normans

Ashmore La

Cocks Rd

Pucks Croft

Faygate Lane

Cobnor

Lambs Green

Stumt Farm

Horsham

5

River Mole

Lambs Green Road

6

Bald Park

Rusper Court House

Axnas Farm

7

Wimland Road

Carylls

8

Coombers Farm

Faygate Lane

Lambs Lane

Kilmwood Lane

Kilmwood

Carylls Lea

Wimlands Lane

A   B   73   C   D   E

H5,H6,H7,K4
Street Names for
these grid squares
are listed at the
back of the index

1 grid square represents 500 metres

F G H 32 J K Holtye

Hammerwood

Brooklands

Hammerwood Park

I

Cansiron Lane

Little Cansiron Farm

2

Owlett's Farm

Great Cansiron Farm

3

Beeches Farm

Thornhill

Surries

4

50

Pollard Wood

North Clays

5

High Weald

Cansiron Lane

6

Lower Parrock

7

Ashdown House

Emerson College

River Medway

8

ablehurst Farm

F G H 82 J K

Medway Drive

HARTFIELD

Stonebarn Cr

Forest

Upper Parrock

Parrock Lane

ROAD

Broadstone

Ashdown Cres

Road

Little Parrock

Forest Way

I grid square represents 500 metres

Fernchase
Manor
F3
1 Bird in Hand St

F4
1 Gromenfield
2 The Homestead

The Green

B7188

LANGTON ROAD

Broom Park

Broomlands

Holmewood Ridge

Ox Lea
slip
Upper
Stephens

Rusthall
Home

F **G** **H** **J** **K**

A264

B2110
Crockers Hatch
Corner

The Hollonds

Broom Lane

Barrow Lane

Hither Chambers

I

F5
1 The Close

Holmewood
House School

GROOMBRIDGE HILL

High Weald Walk

West Walk

PH

Pokehill

River Grom

Spa Valley Railway

Broadwater
Forest

2

3

Newton
Cottages

PO

Station Road

Lealands

Lynwood

St Thomas
C of E
Primary School

High Weald Walk

4

54

5

The
Warren

Birchden

Eridge Road

6

Park Corner

Harrison's
Rocks

Warren
Farm

High Weald Walk

7

Warren Farm
Lane

Forge
Farm

LC

The
Forstal

Hamsell Wood
Farm

8

ott's Farm

F **G** **H** **86** **J** **K**

Eridge
Station

Street Names for these grid squares are listed at the back of the index

F2
1 Broad Gv
2 Clarendon Gdns

G1
1 Cambridge Gdns
2 Clifton Pl
3 Farmcombe Rd
4 Grecian Rd
5 Madeira Pk
6 Norfolk Rd

G2
1 Beau Nash Wy

G3
1 Elphick's Pl

H1
1 Camden Hl
2 Hollyshaw Cl

H3
1 Cypress Gv

J1
1 Camden Pk
2 Hawkenbury Cl
3 Polesden Rd
4 Rookley Cl

J2
1 Hawkenbury Md

F G H J K

I
Lamberhur
A21(T)

Perch Lane
The Gra

2
Clay Hill Cotts

Clay Hill

3

4

5
Hoathly
Farm

6

Clay Hill Road

FURNACE

7
Hook Green

8

Nellis Road

Elmhurst
Farm

Be

Dundale
Farm

Great
Sandhurst
Wood

Dundale Road

Sandhurst
Farm

Kear
Wood

nace
od

Tollsiye

Bayham
Abbey

Bayham
Lake

River Teise

B2169

Little
Bayham

Wickhurst
Farm

Free Heath Road

Kent County
East Sussex County

Mill Road

F G H **90** J K

Stivers
Wood

Bu
Gr

Bartley Mill

Nellis Road

Free

Crowhurst
House

A   B   C   D   E

1   2   3   4   59   5   6   7   8

Critchmere

Shottermill

Camelsdale

Kingsley Green

I grid square represents 500 metres

98

St Marys
C of E First
School
the green
PH
Turners Mead
Pickhurst Road
A283
Hazel
Bridge
Pickhurst Road
High Street Green
High Street Green
Blethwins Farm
High Street
Green
Cherfold
Pickhurst
Follies Farm
Chiddingford
Golf Club
Tugley
Wood
Robins Farm
Fisher Lane
Shillinglee
Park Golf
Club
Fisherlane
Wood
Plaistow Rd
Shillinglee Road
Shillinglee
Home Farm
Shillinglee Road
Gaston's Farm
East
End
Newhouse
Farm
Deer
Tower
Eastland Farm
The
Lake
Haymans Farm

F
G
H
J
K

I
2
3
4
64
5
6
7
8

F
G
H
101
J
K

64

A   B   C   D   E

1 Highstreet
   Green

   Dunsfold
   Ryse

2

3   Tugley
           Wood

           Oaken
           Wood

4   Durfold
                                     Hall Farm

           Fisher Lane   Dungate Farm

63   Dunsfold Road

                                                 Sussex Border Path

5   Fisherlanes   Durfold
           Wood   Wood

                            Sussex Border Path   Durfold

6   Surrey County   Wood

           West Sussex County   Shortland
                                                 Copse

                                                 Weald
                                                 Barkfold

7 Newhouse   East
   Farm   End Farm

8   Lyon's
                                                 Farm

           Haymans Farm   Shillinglee Road

                                                 Dunsfold

   A   B   102   C   D   E

                                                 Road

   Birchfold
   Copse

High Street Green
Chiddington Road   Blacknest Farm   Chiddingfold Road   Wrotham

Plaistow Road

I grid square represents 500 metres

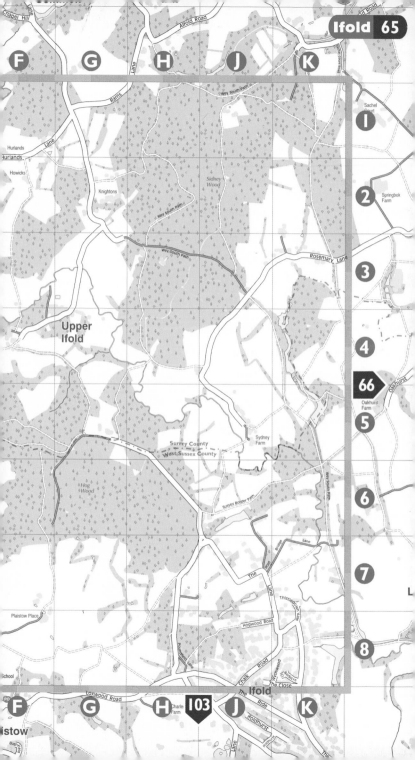

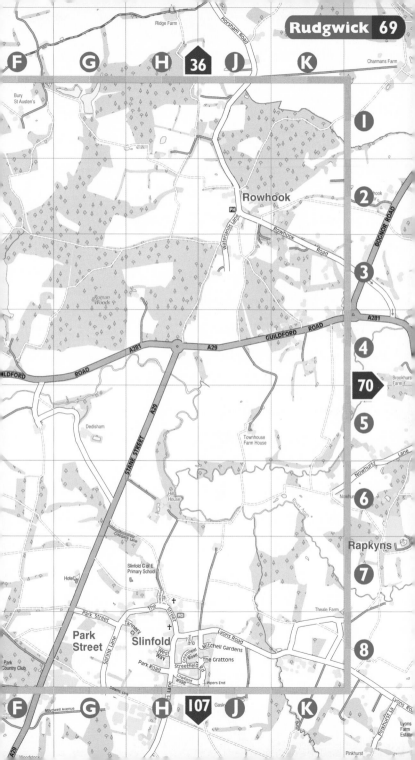

E8
1 Heath Cl
2 St John's Crs

D8
1 Kingsmead Pl
2 Singleton Rd

C8
1 Newbridge Cl

A **B** 37 **C** **D** **E**

Chatfolds

BOGNOR

Warnham
Lodge

Northlands Road

Sands Farm

I

Westbrook
Hall

2
Rowhook
Manor

RH12

Rowhook

Road

Warnham

3

A25

BOGNOR ROAD

The Forge

Tuggles

A281

LDFORD   ROAD

Byfleets Lane

Strood Lane

Ends
Place

4

Brookhurst
Farm

69

Farlington
School

Goosegreen

5

GUILDFORD

**Strood
Green**

Nowhurst   Lane

Byfleets

6

Nowhurst Farm

ROAD

Lane

Broo

River Arun

A281

7

Rapkyns

Old Guildford

Guildford
Road

Broadbridge Heath Road

Theale Farm

Lawson
Hunt Ind
Park

Old Guildford
Road

**Broadbridge
Heath**

A281

St
Primary School

Oak
Lane

Thelton

Swann Way

8

Church Lane

Wickhurst Lane

A Lyons Road **B** 108 **C** **D** **E**

Pinkhurst

Lyons
Farm
Estate

Wellcross
Grange

A264

Broadbridge
Heath Leisure
Centre

A24

Wickhurst Lane

I grid square represents 500 metres

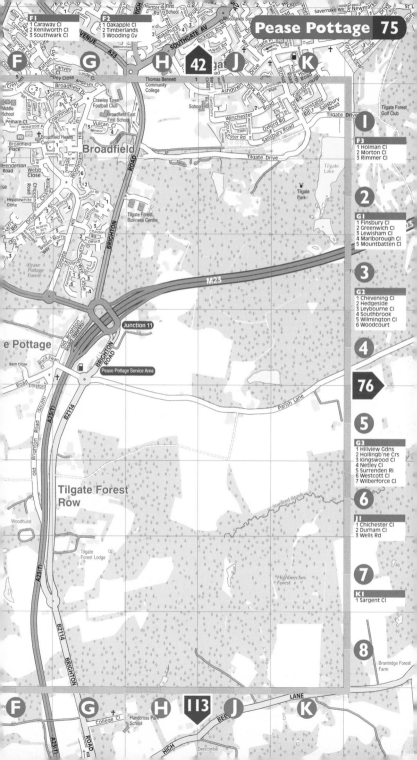

F1
1 Caraway Cl
2 Kenilworth Cl
3 Southwark Cl

F2
1 Oakapple Cl
2 Timberlands
3 Wooding Gv

SOUTHGATE AV

Woodlands Sur

Newmar

savernake Wk

Dickens Road

Wensleydale

Wakehurst

Shepherd

Duxberry

Gossamer

Blackthorn

Canvey Close

A23

Shapley Close

Anglesey Ct

F **G** **H** 42 **J** **K**

Thomas Bennett
Community College

Ashdown

York Road

Salisbury Road

Constable

Salisbury

Calthorpe Road

Barn

Canterbury

Tilgate Forest
Golf Club

I

F3
1 Holman Cl
2 Morton Cl
3 Rimmer Cl

2

Tilgate Lake

Tilgate Park

G1
1 Finsbury Cl
2 Greenwich Cl
3 Lewisham Cl
4 Marlborough Cl
5 Mountbatten Cl

3

M23

G2
1 Chevening Cl
2 Hedgeside
3 Leybourne Cl
4 Southbrook
5 Wilmington Cl
6 Woodcourt

Junction 11

4

Barn Close

Black Swan

Pease Pottage Service Area

76

BRIGHTON ROAD

Parish Lane

5

G3
1 Hillview Gdns
2 Hollingb'ne Crs
3 Kingswood Cl
4 Netley Cl
5 Surrenden Ri
6 Westcott Cl
7 Wilberforce Cl

6

Tilgate Forest
Row

Stanford Brook

J1
1 Chichester Cl
2 Durham Cl
3 Wells Rd

Woodhurst

Tilgate
Forest Lodge

Highbeeches
Forest

7

K1
1 Sargent Cl

8

Brantridge Forest
Farm

College Cl

Handcross Park
School

BEE LANE

F **G** **H** 113 **J** **K**

HIGH

Dencombe

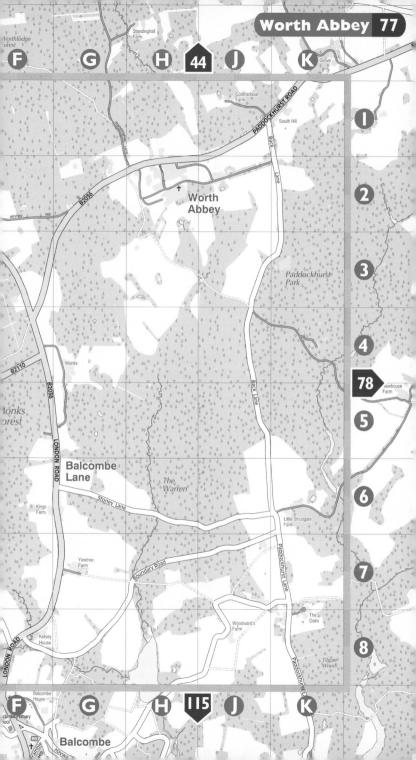

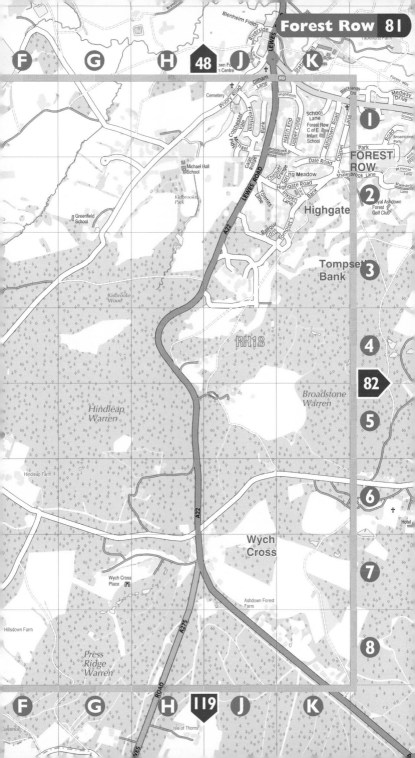

F G H **48** J K

Blenheim Fields
Riverside
LEWES
Tablehurst Farm
Forest Row Ha
Station

I
Medway Drive
Broadstone Park
School Lane
FOREST ROW
Park Road
Primrose Way
Shalesbro Lane

Cemetery
Priory Road
Gilham Lane
Freshfield Bank
Highfields
Hatch End
Upper Close
Ashdown Road
Chapel Lane
Forest Row C of E Infant School

Colchester Vale
Michael Hall
Castle Ridge
Chequer Grange
Woodcock
Dale Road
Shalesbrook Lane

Michael Hall School
ng Meadow
Highgate Road
Imxen Lane
Bank

2
Royal Ashdown Forest Golf Club

Kidbrooke Park
Forests Lane
Highgate

Greenfield School
Balfour Cdns
Tompsett's

Tompset Bank **3**

Kidbrooke Wood

RH18

4

82

Hindleap Warren

Broadstone Warren

5

Hindleap Farm

6
Hotel

Wych Cross

7

Wych Cross Place

Ashdown Forest Farm

Hillsdown Farm

8

Press Ridge Warren

A275

A22

F G H **119** J K

Isle of Thorns
ommon
LEWES ROAD

Emerson College

River Medway

Tablehurst Farm

A   B   49   C   D   E

Forest Row Business Park

Station Road

Forest Row Business Park

Blacklands Crs

Forest Way

Medway Drive

Stonedene Dr

HARTFIELD

Park Crs

ROAD

Forest Way

Upper Parrock

Parrock Lane

School Lane

Forest C of E Infant School

Ashdown Rd

Chapel Lane

Hatch End

Upper Close

Dale Road

Park

FOREST ROW

Ashdown Rd

Broadstone Pars

Highfield

Stonepark Dr

Horn Lane

1

Little Parrock

Forest Road

River

Wood

Road

2 Highgate

Bank

Shalesbrook Lane

Primrose Lane

Shalesbrook Lane

Royal Ashdown Forest Golf Club

Vanguard Way

Quabrook

Coleman Hatch

SHEPHERD'S

HILL

Holli

3 Tempset's Bank

River Medway

River Medway

4

Broadstone Farm

The Ridge

81

Bro
Warren

5

Sandy Lane

Vanguard Way

M

Colemans Hatch Road

6

Hotel

†

†

7

8

Ash Down

A   B   120   C   D   E

Pippingford Park

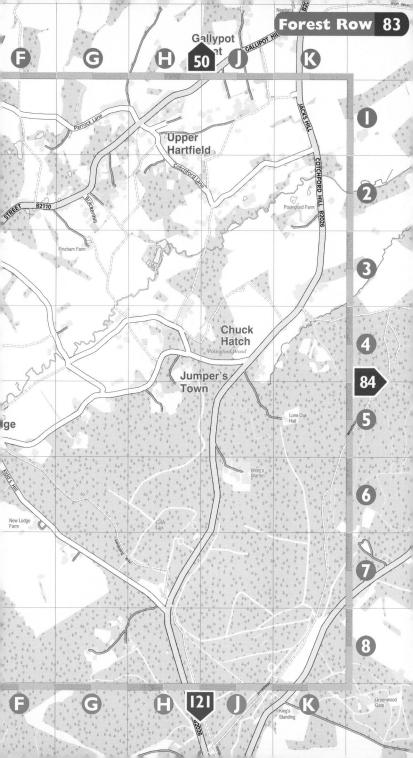

F   G   H   50   J   K

Newton's

Gallypot

GALLIPOT HILL

JACKS HILL

COTCHFORD HILL B2026

high Weald

Parrock Lane

Upper Hartfield

Cotchford Lane

STREET   B2110

Brackenhill

Posingford Farm

Fincham Farm

Chuck Hatch

Posingford Wood

Jumper's Town

Lone Oak Hall

lge

King's Hill

New Lodge Farm

Gills Lap

Wren's Warren

84

Westerway

Greenwood Gate

King's Standing

F   G   H   121   J   K

B2026

I   2   3   4   5   6   7   8

H7
1 Gillridge Gn

H8
1 Elphick Pl
2 Mill Crs
3 Park Crs

F G H 52 J Mott's Mill K

I

J8
1 The Farthings
2 Sefton Wy

2

Corseley Road

Leyswood

High Weald Landscape Trail

Penns in
the Rocks

B2188

Lye
Green

Park
Grove

3

Trail

Littlebrook

Bream Wood

Orznash
Farm

4

86

Gillridge
Farm

5
Boarshead

Beecher
Wood

6

Toadley Lane

Smugglers Lane

7

Innham's Wood

Coopers
Wood

Norbury
Close

Ashleigh
Gdns

Pleasant View
Road

Connell
Wood

Hourne Farm

ERIDGE ROAD

n's

Coopers
Lane

Civil

Ellison
Close

Elm Ct

London Road

Pinner

Goldsmith
Leisure
Centre

8

High
Cross Fields

Steel
Cross

GREEN LANE

B26

Glenmore Road
East

Beacon Rd West

Beacon Gardens

Avenue

Sheiling
Road

Highlands
Close

Doctors
Surgery

Hotel

Grove

THE BROADWAY

HIGH

Wealden
Close

Setton

Eridge Drive

Mill
Road

Millbrook

Oldhurst
Drive

Charity
Farm
Way

Barnfield

HOLLYWOOD Close

Beacon
Community
College

B2157

F G H 123 J K Poundfield

Woodside

B26

Mill

Pine Road

Saxonborough
Surgery

Saxonbury
Close

Church Road

St Marys
Primary
Catholic School

Fermor
School

Beacon
Community
College

Poundfield

F   G   H   54   J   K

High Weald Walk

I

Forge Wood

2

Danegate

Sussex Border Path

3

Pococksgate

Stonewall

4

88

Great Danegate

5

Saxonbury Farm

Green Hedges Farm

6

Brickyard Lane

Moth Wood

Entry Hill

Forest Farm

7

Mark Cross

Greenhouse Farm

Mark Cross C of E School

8

F   G   H   125   J   K

B2100

Heathfield

MAYFIELD

Brickdon Hill

Thornhurst Road

F   G   H   **56**   J   K

I

2

3

Barelands Farm

Camden Wood

Great Shoesmiths Farm

Sussex Border Path

Henley Wood

B2099

Lane

Dewhurst Lodge

Dewhurst Lane

Sussex Border Path

White Gates Farm

Whitegates Lane

4

Riverhall

Tappington Farm

Sussex Border Path

Rockrobin

Three Oaks Lane

90 Tun Gre

Wadhurst Business Park

STATION ROAD

B2099

Buckhurst Lane

Wadhurst Station

5

The Mounts

Mount School

Sussex Border Path

Durgates Industrial Estate

HIGH STREET

6

Buckhurst Place

Faircrouch Lane

Tapsell's Lane

Mayfield Park

Durgates

Sussex Border Path

Ravensdale Farm

Sacred Heart School

Ward Close

Walk

Castle

Turnmill Lane

7

Bird Lane

Beggars Bush

Buckhurst Lane

Fairglen Road

Faircrouch Lane

MAYFIELD

LANE

B2100

Bellerbys College Mayfield

Best Beech Hill

8

Skinner's Farm

HURST   ROAD

Foxes Bank

F   G Pennybridge   H   **127**   J   K

Riseden

Snape Wood

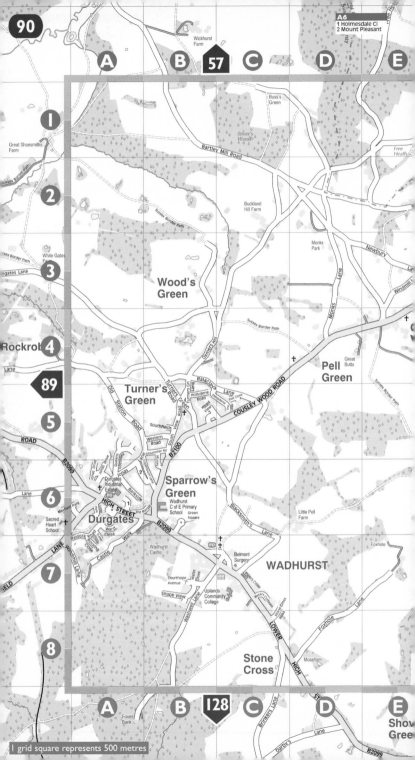

F G H The Down J K

Neills Road

Furnace Avenue

E SLADE

A21(1)

Owls Castle Farm

Hoghole Lane

Sweetbridge Lane

B2100

Wisketts Wood

Bexhill

Bewbridge Lane

I

Kent County
East Sussex County

2

Markwicks

3

COUSLEY WOOD ROAD

Ladymeads Farm

Hook Farm

Lower
Cousley Wood

Sussex Border Path

Bewl Water

4

92

Little Butts Farm

Bryant's Farm

Beaumans

5

Ward's Lane

Hook Hill

Clapham Lane

6

Sussex Border Path

Chesson's Farm

Lower Hazelhurst

7

Whilligh

Lower Hazelhurst

Rowley

8

Ward's Lane

Birchetts Green Lane

Pinion Hill

**Birchett's
Green**

Lane

F G H **129** J K

Holbeam Wood

Tolhurst

Birchetts Green Lane

Lodge Lane

Broomden

Vineyard Lane

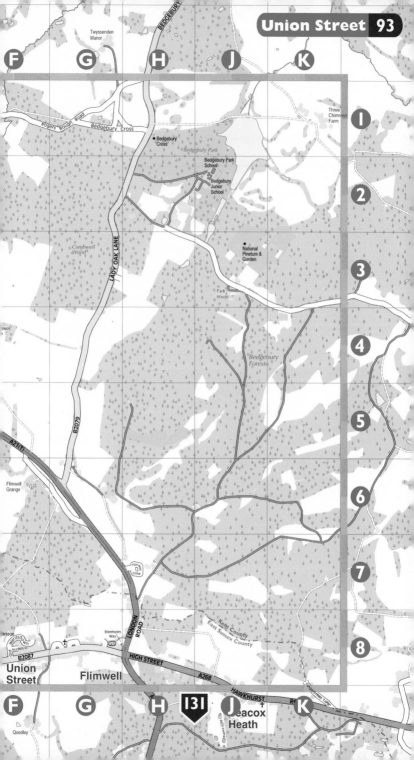

F   G   H   J   K

Twyssenden Manor

BEDGEBURY

Three Chimneys Farm

I

Rogers Rough Road   Bedgebury Cross

• Bedgebury Cross

Bedgebury Park

2

Bedgebury Park School

Bedgebury Junior School

Combwell Wood

LADY OAK LANE

• National Pinetum & Garden

3

Park House

4

Bedgebury Forest

B2079

5

A2100

Flimwell Grange

6

7

Old Nursery Cl

Turn Cross

Kent County
East Sussex County

8

Quedley

B2087   Old Road

LONDON ROAD

Blenheim Way

HIGH STREET

A268

HAWKHURST

Gillbrook Lane

Union Street   **Flimwell**   **I31**   **Peacox Heath**

F   G   H   J   K

F G H J K

Old Thorns Golf
& Country Club

Queen's Road

I

Foley
Manor

2

Wheatsheaf
Common

Forest
Mere

Sussex Border Path

3

PORTSMOUTH RD

Liphook
Golf
Club

Home
Park

Sussex Border Path

4

B??

Ripsley House

gley

Langley
Court

96

5

Milland House

Sussex Border Path

Chapel
Common

6

Milland Lane

County

Rakes
Firs

✝

7

Rake C of E
Controlled
First School

Maysleith

Maysleith
Wood

8

F G H **136** J K Mi

Godning

Great
Trippetts Farm

Rake Road

Chorley
Common

Cane

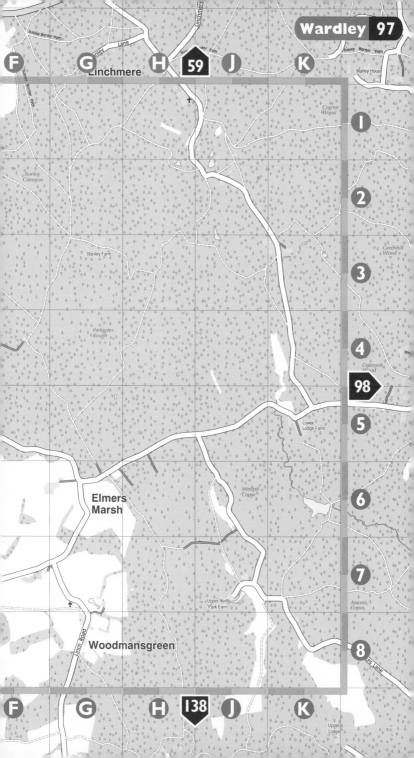

Sussex Border Path

Stanley Lane

Linchmere

Sussex Border Path

F G H **59** J K

Marley House

Sussex Border Path

I

Cognor Wood

Stanley Common

2

Greenhill Wood

Stanley Farm

3

Parkgate Rough

4

Oakreeds Wood

98

Lower Lodge Farm

5

Elmers Marsh

Minepit Copse

6

7

Anon's Copse

Upper North Park Farm

Linch Road

Woodmansgreen

8

Forest Lane

F G H **I38** J K

Upper Lodge

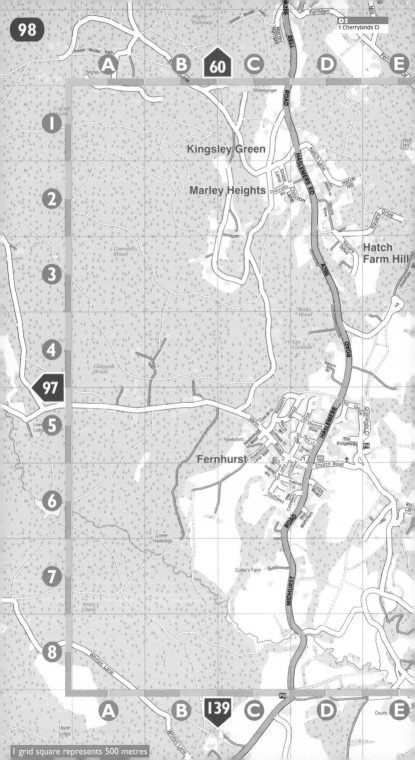

98

A B **60** C D E

1 Cherrylands Cl

I

Colnor Wood

Kingsley Green

2

Marley Heights

Hatch Farm Hill

3

Greenhill Wood

4

Oakreeds Wood

97

Reeks Wood

Van Common

5

Low Lodge

Hawksford

Fernhurst

The Ridgeway

Church Road

6

Lower Hawksford

7

Collier's Farm

Amen's Copse

8

Whites Lane

A B **139** C D E

Upper Lodge

Courts

1 grid square represents 500 metres

F G H 61 J K

Surrey County
West Sussex County

Home
Wood

sussex Border path

Chase Lane

Valewood Ho

Ferndan Lane

Black
Down

Silver Border Path

Cotchet Farm

280
Blackdown Hill

Ferndan Lane

Reeth

Ferndan Lane

Blackdown
Farm

Leazers
Wood

Lower
House Farm

Hammonds
Copse

Aldworth Ho

Roundhurst
Farms

Abeslers

Tennyson's Lane

Jay's Lane

Roundhurst
Common

Jobson's Lane

100

Shopp
Hill

Windfallwood
Common

Great
Brockhurst
Farm

Dial
Green

Highstead Lane

Hursfold Farm

F G H 140 J K

ck Fa

Lower
Gentlishurst
Farm

I 1 2 3 4 5 6 7 8

F G H **63** J K

Haymans Farm
estland Farm

The Lake

Park Mill Farm

I

Frith Wood

2

Dale's Farm

Mitchell Park Farm

3

Piper's Copse

ars Lane

ers Lane

4

Hortons Farm

apel

102

Fisherd Farm

5

Freehold Farm

6

Hig

Pheasant Court Farm

Street's Lane

Ebernoe

7

Pl

Willand Wood

Ebernoe Common

8

Butcherland Farm

F G H **142** J K

Colhook Common

High Buildings Farm

A   B   64   C   D   E

I

Haymans Farm

Birchfold Copse

Lyon's Farm
Shillinglee Road
Dunsfold Road
Oakfield

2

Dale's Farm

Rumbolds Farm

3

Upper Frithfold Farm

Piper's Copse

4

Piper's Lane

Roundwyck House

101

Frithfold Farm

5

Howick

6

Scratchings Lane
Scratchings Farm

Highncions Farm

Scratchings Lane

Streel's Lane

Ebernoe

Piper's Lane

7

Hall Green Farm

Beal House Farm

Hoe Bridge

8

Ebernoe Common

Butcherland Farm

St

A   B   143   C   D   E

High Buildings Farm

Allfields Farm

1 grid square represents 500 metres

F **G** **H** 67 **J** **K**

Garlands

I

PH

2

3

4

106

5

Great Wood

6

7 Okehurst Lane
Copped Hall
Farm

8

F **G** **H** 146 **J** **K**
Tedfold

Gibbons
Mill

Drungewick
Manor

Drungewick Lane

Okehurst Road

Martel Lane

Hope
Farm

Bignor
Farm

Okehurst Road

Malham

Wey-South Path

Okehurst

Wey-South Path

Loves Farm

**Newpound
Common**

River Arun

Wey and Arun Canal

Paplands Farm

Rowner

NEWPOUND

Newpound Lane

Fishers Farm Park

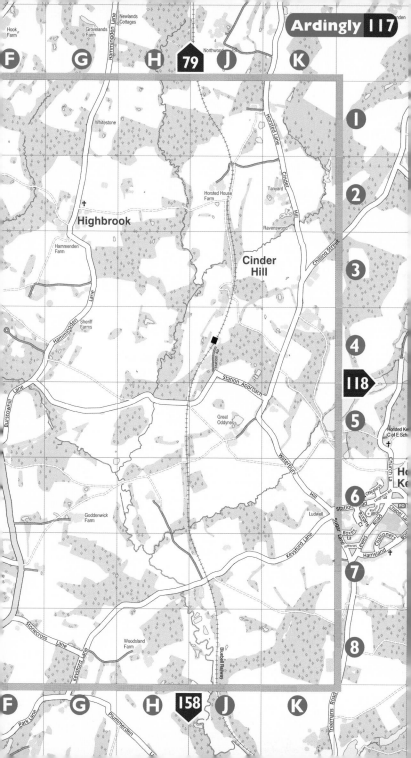

F G H 79 J K

I

2

3

4

118

5

6

7

8

Hook Farm

Newlands Cottages

Grovelands Farm

Whitestone

Highbrook

Hammenden Farm

Horsted House Farm

Tanyard

Ravenswood

Cinder Hill

Sheriff Farms

Great Oddynes

Ludwell

Goddenwick Farm

Burstowhill Lane

Station Approach

Station Road

Keysford Lane

Hammenden Lane

Stonecross Lane

Keysford Lane

Woodsland Farm

Part Lane

Plummerden

Horsted Lane

Cinder Hill

Chilling Street

Northwood

Horsted Keynes C of E Sch

Church La

Chelsey's

Horsted Keynes

Lewes Road

Box La

Jefferies

Chaloners

Hamsland

Sugar Lane

Bluebell Railway

Treemans Road

F G H 158 J K

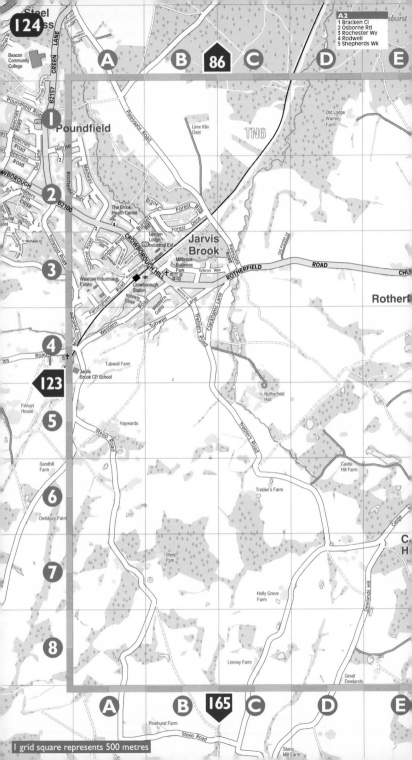

F G H 89 J K

I
Foxes
Bank
Snape Wood

Beggars Bush
Farlands
Farleigh
B216
College
Mayfield
Best B

HURST
ROAD

Pennybridge

Riseden

Snape House

2
Snape Lane

3

Snape
Farm

Riseden

Road

Tidebrook

Tidebrook
Manor

Coombe
Lane

Coombe

4

128

Lodge
Hill Farm

Chittinghurst

Rusher's
Cross

Tide Brook

Combe

5

Cinderhill
Farm

6

Combe
Wood

Sharnden
Old Manor
Farm

7

8

Merrieweathers

Roll's
Farm

F G H 168 J K

Hawksden
Park
Wood

Hare
Holt

A **B** 90 **C** **D** **E**

Foxes
Bank

Snape Wood

Show
Gree

Brinkers Lane

Darby's

Lane

B2099

+

I

Snape House

2

Walland
Manor

Snape Lane

Snape
Farm

3

Wenbans

Scrag
Oak

The
Olives

Road

Lane

Churchsettle Lane

4

Buttons

Churchsettle
Farm

127

5

Wadhurst
Park

Flattenden
Farm

6

Dens
Farm

Wadhurst Park
Lake

7

Batt's
Wood

8

Newbridge
Wood

River Rother

A **B** 169 **C** **D** **E**

Bivelham Forge
Farm

I grid square represents 500 metres

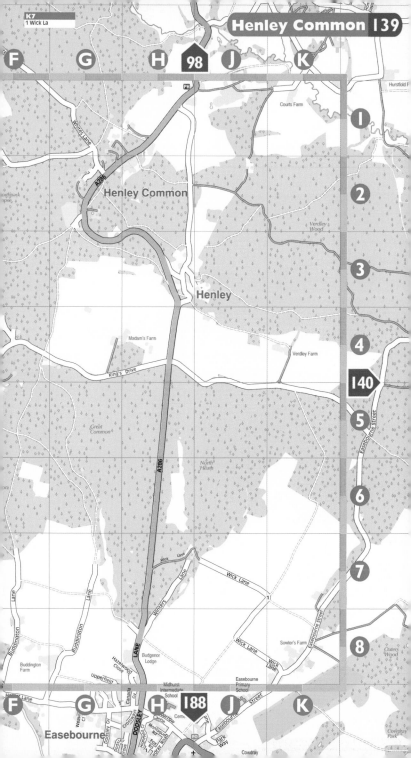

F G H 100 J K

Park Farm

PH
PO
Lurgashall

Gatehouse Farm

I

2

Old
Mill Farm

Mill Pond

3

Stagpark Farm

Mill Farm

White's
Green

4

142

River Park Farm

5

Parkhurst
Farm

Lord's
Wood

6

Copse Lane

7

Westland's

Salmonsbridge Farm

River
Common

Uppertin
Common

8

River Lane

James Lane

F G Riv H 190 J Pitshill K New Road Upper

River Lane

Brookwell Lane

Dene Dan

F G H 102 J K

I

2

3

4

144

5

6

7

8

F G H 192 J K

Butcherland Farm

Parsonage

igh
uildings Farm

Allfields Farm

**Balls
Cross**

Sladelands

Pipers Lane

Crawfold
Farm

Langhurst Farm

Medhone
Farm

Blackhouse Lane

Holland
Wood

Blackbrook Farm

Bennyfold Farm

Pondtail
Copse

ge

Moor Farm

Beechfield

Blackhouse Lane

HORSHAM   ROAD   A272   A272

Hilliers

144

Staples Hill

Parsonage Farm

Great Common

Boxalland Farm

A B 103 C D E

Kirdford

Kirdford County Junior School

PH

Slade lands

Crawfold Farm

1

2

Linfold Farm

Gownfold Farm

3

Gandersgate Lane

Medhone Farm

4

143

Brownings

5

Marshall's Farm

Strood

6

Bennyfold Farm

Glasshouse Lane

7

Crimbourne Lane

The Adens

Nature Reserve

Battlehurst Farm

The Cut

8

A272

Hawkhurst Court

A Beechfield B 193 C D E

A272

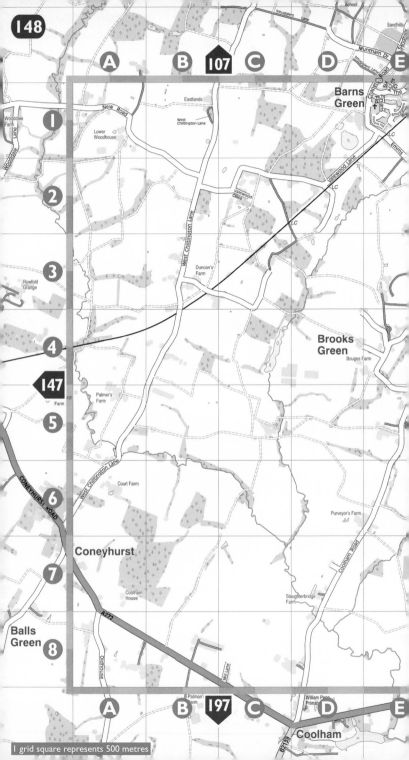

Barns Green 149

Southwater Street

F **G** **H** ◣108 **J** **K**

Watlings Farm

Blakes

Nyes Lane

Green Close

Great House Farm

Copse

The Lawns

Southwater County Junior Infant School

I

Pye Lane
Richmond Farm
Two Mile Ash Road

Two Mile Ash Road

Woodgate

Church Lane

The Forge

Quarry

Timber

Church Lane

Oak Rd

Station

2

Industrial Estate

Southwater Business Park

Amber Gdns

Ash Road

College Road

Chase Farm

Shaws Lane

Southwater Country Park

Southwater

3

Woodlands Way

Beechwood

Maripost Wood

Maripost Road

The Oaks

Foxe

Andrews Rd

Mill

Little Str

Wessex

Rascals

Netherwood

Oak Close

4

Rascals

Close

◣150

Lane

Netherwoods Road

5

Shipley Road

Woodgetters

Dragons Green Road

Trawler's Farm

Brick Kiln Farm

6

Baker's Farm

Goffsland Farm

7

Bakers Lane

Dragons Green Road

Dragons Lane

PH

8

Dragons Green

Green Street

F **G** **H** ◢198 **J** **K** A272

Butterstocks Farm

F G H **110** J K

I
2
3
4
152
5
6
7
8

Saxton's Farm

Newells Farm

Sedgwick Park

Nuthurst

St Andrews C of E (aided) School

Harriots Close

Micklepage Farm

Gaveston Hall

Maplehurst

Park Lane

Park Lane

Woldringfold

Brook Farm

Conies Farm

Ivorys

Joles Farm

Smallham Farm

Belmoredean

Home Farm

Capons Hill Farm

Browning's

Clock House

Capon's Farm

St Peters C Primary Sch

F G H **200** J A272 K

BROWNING'S HILL A272

A272

Nuthurst St

Nuthurst Road

Maplehurst Road

Prings Lane

Peacock's Hill

Burnthouse Lane

Newells Lane

Copsale Road

Kennel Lane

Burnthouse Lane

I grid square represents 500 metres

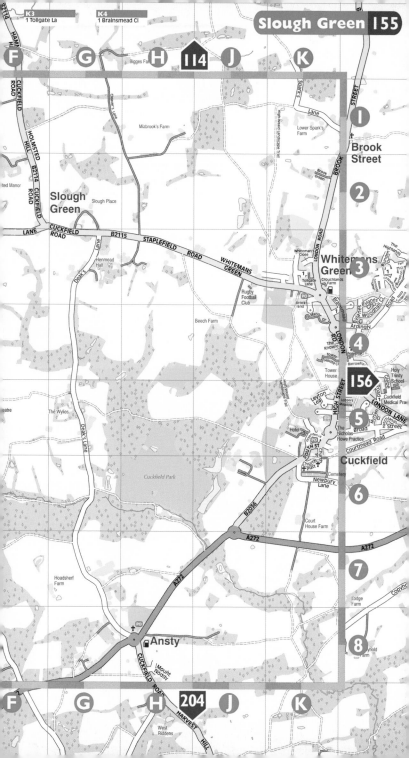

F7
1 Fairbanks
2 Highland Ct
3 Iona Wy

F8
1 Ashenground Cl

G3
1 Barrington Wd
2 Portsmouth Wd

G6
1 Little Bentswood
2 Marylands

G7
1 Bluebell Cl
2 Firlands
3 Mayflower Ct
4 Strathfield Cl

G8
1 Oakdale Rd
2 Swainsthorpe Cl

H3
1 Denman's Cl

H6
1 Langridge La

H7
1 The Oaks

H8
1 Frankton Av
2 Woodridge Cl

J3
1 Hickman's Cl

F6
1 The Rushes

G5
1 Kidbrook

J7
1 Catkin Wy
2 Rushwood Cl
3 Walnut Pk

J6
1 Coombers La
2 Rustlings Cl

Lindfield

HAYWARDS HEATH

RH16

116

158

206

F G H 118 J K

159

I
2
3
4
160 Sheffield Green
5
6
7
8

Freshfield Lane

Birch Lane

ROAD
A275

Latchetts

Stoaches Farm

Danehurst

Northlands Farm

Glenmore Farm

Slider's Lane

Freshfield Crossways

Freshfield Lane

Town Place

Ketche's Lane

Sussex Border Path

Slider's Lane

Ketche's Farm

Ketche's Lane

Sheffield Green

Bluebell Railway

PH

Sheffield Bridge

Butterbox Lane

Massetts

Sennolls Farm

Wapsbourne Farm

A275

F G H 208 J K

Lindfield Farm

Warr's Farm

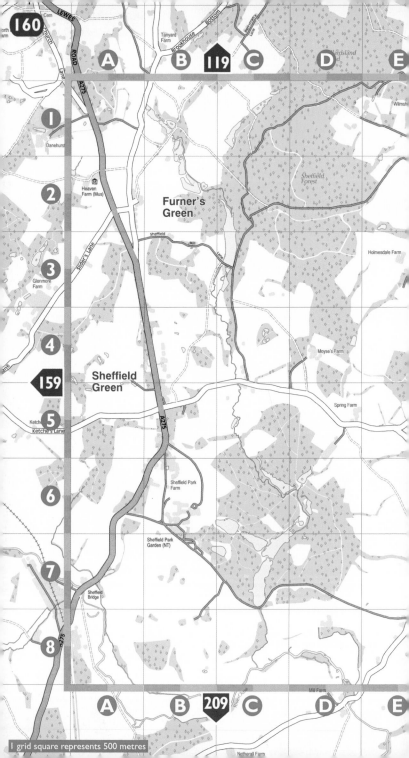

Nutley

Ford's Green

Prickets Hatch

Funnell's Farm

Hunters Farm

Woodcock Farm

Searles

Down Street

Black Ven Farm

Picketts Lane

Horney Common

Castle Street

Dodd's Bank

Courtlands

Cackle Street

Tiers Lane

Old Lane

Clapwater House

Ruttingham Farm

High Wood

Splayne's Green

Down Street

Mallingdown Farm

Down Street

Grover's

The Piltdown Golf Club

Nether Lane

Forest View

STREET

A22

A272

Colliers Drive

120

162

210

F G H J K

1

2

3

4

5

6

7

8

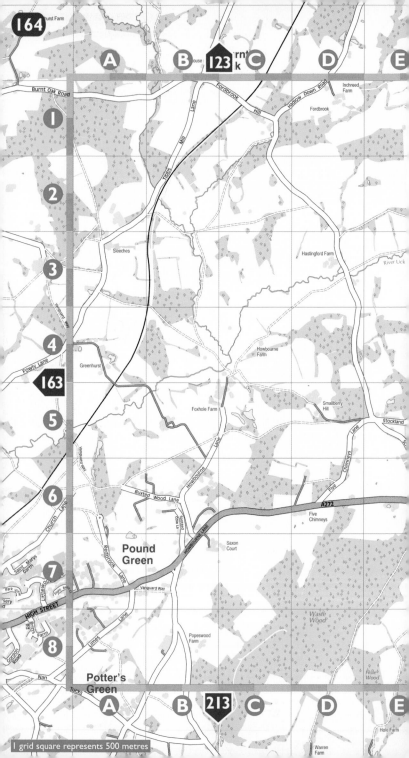

F   G   H   124   J   K

Limney F.

Great Dewlands

Streel Farm

I

Pinehurst Farm

Steep Road

2

Stone Mill Farm

Devlands Hill

Stonehurst

Huggett's Furnace

Stockyards Farm

Woodreed Farm

Stonehurst

3

Skippers Hill Manor Preparatory School

A267

Skippers Hill

4

Stonehurst Lane

Broadreed Farm

Criers Lane

Queensmount

166

...nes ...ary ... School

A267

Pigsfoot Farm

Kiln Lane

Little Broadreed Farm

5

Boltons Clinic

Brick Lane

Lane

Wheelers

Dog Kennel Lane

Frog

Hol

Hadlow Down

Hadlow House

Poundford

6

Hall Lane

A272

Hodges

ss Lane

Wilderness Wood

Tinker's Lane

Little England Farm

A267

7

Loudwell Farm

Coles Hall

Wilderness Farm

8

Mercs

F   G   H   214   J   K

Spood's F.

Scocus Wood

Dudsland Farm

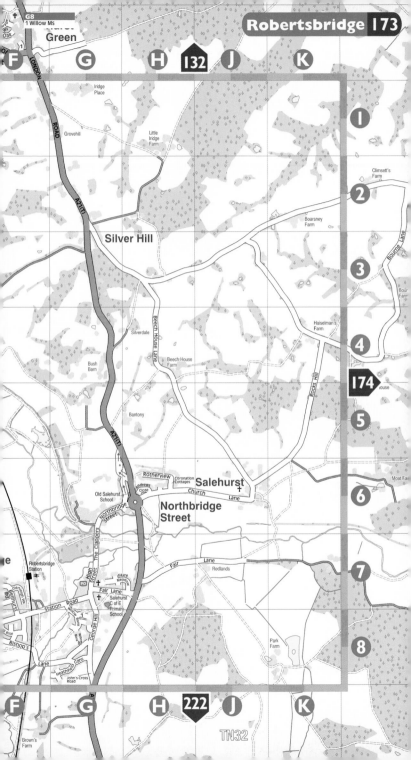

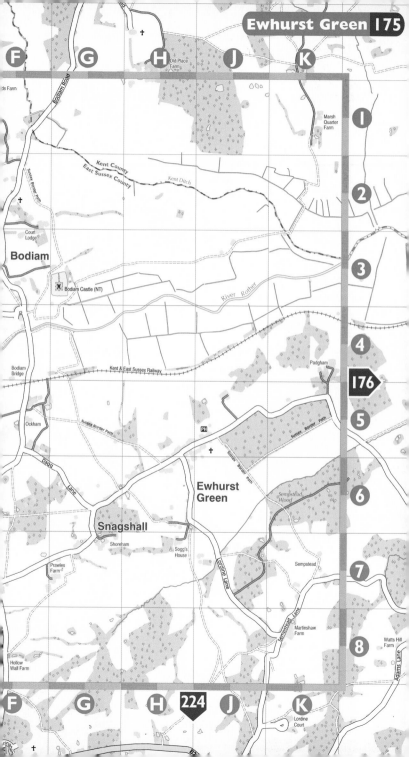

F G H J K

I

Old Place Farm

Marsh Quarter Farm

Bodiam Road

2

Kent County
East Sussex County

Kent Ditch

Sussex Border Path

3

Court Lodge

Bodiam

Bodiam Castle (NT)

River Rother

4

Padgham

176

Bodiam Bridge

Kent & East Sussex Railway

5

Ockham

Sussex Border Path

Sussex Border Path

Dagg Lane

PH

Sempstead Wood

6

Ewhurst Green

Snagshall

Shoreham

Sogg's House

Lordine Lane

Sempstead

7

Prawles Farm

Sempstead Lane

Martinshaw Farm

8

Watts Hill Farm

Hollow Wall Farm

Adams Lane

F G H **224** J K

Lordine Court

F G H J K

Wittersham

Swan Street
Swan Street
Swan Cottages
Forge Reach
POPLAR
B2082 STOCKS ROAD

Cemetery
Street
The
Wittersham Primary School

Wittersham Manor

Blackbrook Farm

Budd's Reach

I

Ham Green

Budd's Farm

2

Kent County
East Sussex County

3

Sussex Border Path

Kitchenham

Sussex Border Path

4

180 179

5
Farm

Readers Lane

6

Moat Farm

Forstal Farm

7
Coldharbour

Old House Farm

Iden Wood

8

F G H 228 J K

A268
MAIN

Malthouse Business Park
The Old Hop Garden

Farleys Way

Peasmarsh

STREET
Lane

A268 RYE

Brabands

Lane

F G H J K

Oxenden

Mackley Farm

Church Hill

Military Road

Royal Military Canal

Highknock

Knock Hill

Stone Bridge

Cliff Farm

Stone Cliff

Cliff Marsh Farm

Saxon Shore Way

Royal Military Canal Path

Royal Military Canal

Five Watering Sewer

White Kemp Sewer

Military Road

Saxon Shore Way

East Sussex County

Kent County

FOLKESTONE ROAD

Offen's Farm

A259(T)

Lamb Farm

Guldeford Lane Corner

LC

F G H 230 J K

I
2
3
4
5
6
7
8

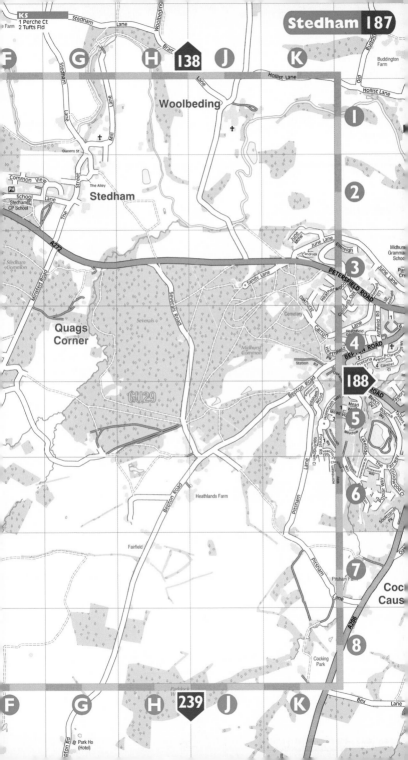

KS
1 Perche Ct
2 Tufts Fld

F **G** **H** **138** **J** **K**

Stedham Lane

Woolbeding

Buddington
Farm

Hollist Lane

Hollist Lane

I

Woolbeding

Queens St

2

Common View

PH

School
Stedham
CP School

The Street

Stedham

The Alley

June
Way

Elmleigh

June Lane

Midhurst
Grammar
Schoo

A272

Minsted Road

Stedham
Common

Severals

Severals Road

Sandy Lane

Cemetery

Oakhurst

PETERSFIELD ROAD

Heatherwood

Guildford Rd

Carron

Lane

Heathfield

3

June Lane

Ashfield Rd

Pa
Cro

1
6

**Quags
Corner**

Midhurst
Common

Station Rd

Heathfield
Pk

BELL ROAD

Pretoria Avenu

Clarence
Cavalie
Ct

4

GU29

Bepton Road

Fosters

188

Mead

ROAD

5

Hopmedow Way

Mead Wa

1
2

Meadow

Beac
Cotl
Bourne
Wl

Heathlands Farm

Bepton Road

Forest
Rd
Southdown Cl

Hawt

Lakeside

The
Fairwa
Woodway

6

Pitsham

Lane

Kew
Poplar

Southamp
Pk

Fairfield

7

Pitsham
Lane

Pitsham Fam

Coc
Caus

A286

Cocking
Park

8

Padd
W

F **G** **H** **239** **J** **K**

Bex
Lane

Park Ho
(Hotel)

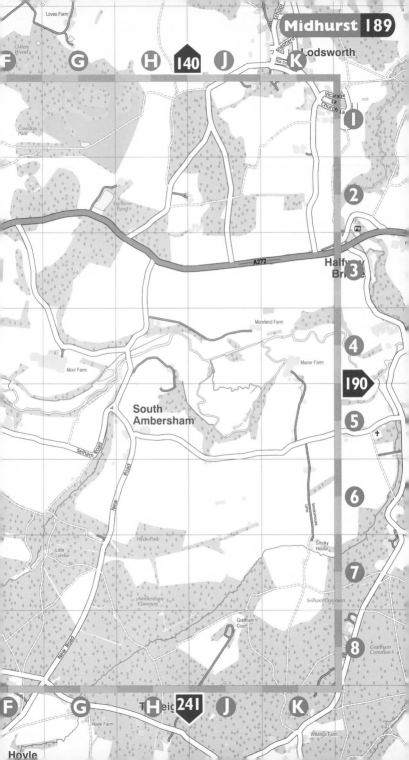

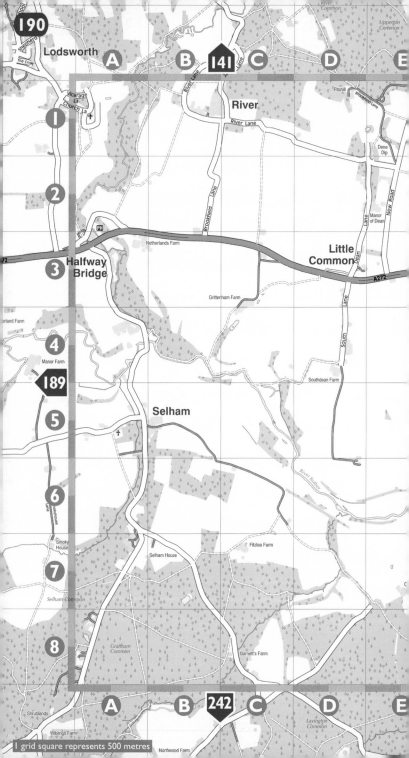

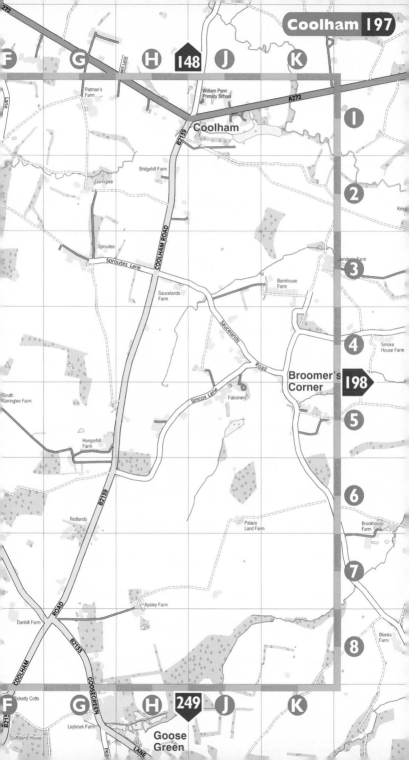

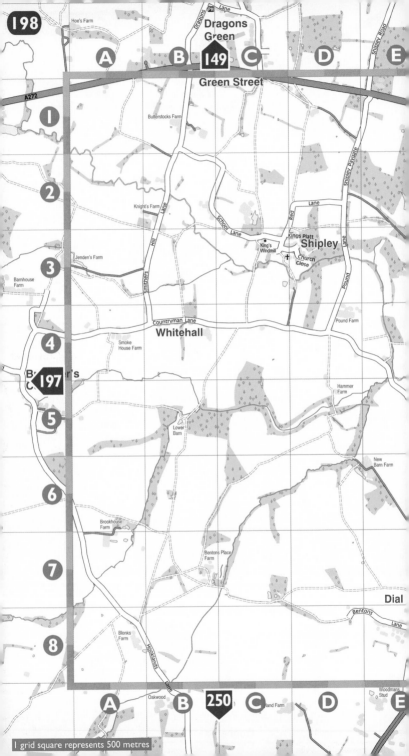

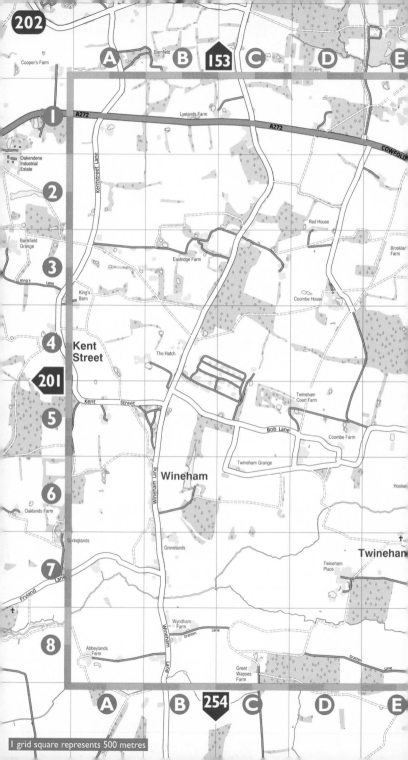

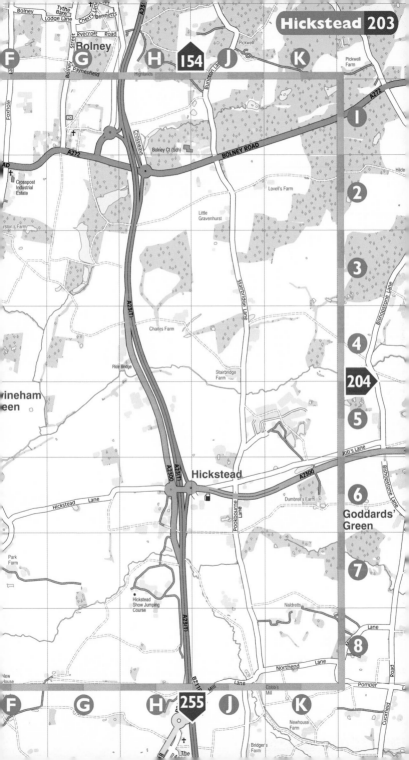

E7
1 Baylis Crs
2 Pannett
3 Wallis Wy
4 Withy Bush

E6
1 Withy Bush

D7
1 Chaffinch Cl

155

Ansty

A   B   C   D   E

I

West Riddens

Harvesthill

E8
1 Colmer Pl
2 Victoria Av
3 Victoria Cl
4 Weald Rd

Pickwell Farm

Lovell's Farm

2

Hilders Farm

Legh Manor

3

Greenacres

Lye's Farm

Paynes Place Farm

4

203

Abbotsf

5

Job's Lane

6

A2300

A2300

A273 S

Dumbrell's F.

Goddards' Green

Bretton

7

Oaklands Park

Naldretts

8

Lane

Mill Lane

Northend Lane

Pomper Lane

Southway County Junior School

Southway

A   B   C   D   E

256

Kent's Farm

Newhouse Farm

Victoria

Jubilee Road

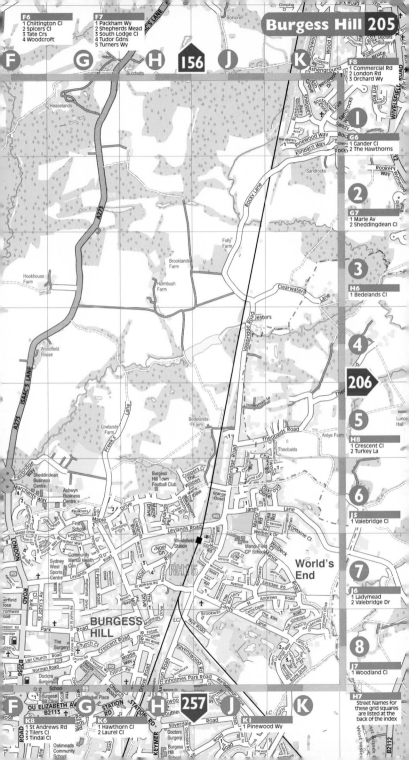

F6
1 Chiltington Cl
2 Spicers Cl
3 Tate Crs
4 Woodcroft

F7
1 Packham Wy
2 Shepherds Mead
3 South Lodge Cl
4 Tudor Gdns
5 Turners Wy

F8
1 Commercial Rd
2 London Rd
3 Orchard Wy

G6
1 Gander Cl
2 The Hawthorns

G7
1 Marle Av
2 Sheddingdean Cl

H6
1 Bedelands Cl

H8
1 Crescent Cl
2 Turkey La

J5
1 Valebridge Cl

J6
1 Ladymead
2 Valebridge Dr

J7
1 Woodland Cl

H7
Street Names for these grid squares are listed at the back of the index

K8
1 St Andrews Rd
2 Tilers Cl
3 Tindal Cl

K6
1 Hawthorn Cl
2 Laurel Cl

K1
1 Pinewood Wy

F G H **158** J K

Scaynes
Hill

A272

Awbrook

Vicarage Lane

Church Road

Ham Lane

Hillcrest Lane

Sunnycroft
Close

Hooklands
Farm

Inces

Pellingbridge
Farm

Hammond's
Farm

Vale
Farm

Great
Noven
Farm

1

2

West Sussex County
East Sussex County

3

Teague's
Farm

Leylands
Farm

LEWES ROAD

A272

4

Holford
Manor

Old
Her
Chailey
Heritage
School

208

BEGGAR'S

5

Wivelsden
Farm

North Common Road

Broadstone
Farm

6

Newhouse
Farm

Longridge

Townings
Farm

Common Road

Godleys
Green

Breens
Cottages

Hole Farm

7

8

Bower Farm

F G H **259** J K

Heath
Farm

The
Hooke

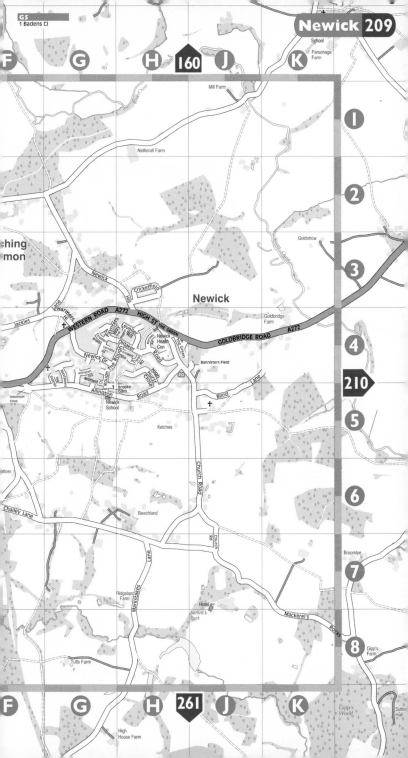

G5
1 Badens Cl

F G H 160 J K

Newick

I
2
3
4
210
5
6
7
8

Mill Farm

Netherall Farm

Goldstrow

hing
mon

Newick

Cricketfield

Hill

Harmers

Jackles

WESTERN ROAD A272 HIGH ST THE GREEN

Levellr
Rd

Painters

Newick
Health
Cen

Goldbridge
Farm

GOLDBRIDGE ROAD A272

Newick Dr

The Rough

Allington Road

Newick
School

Brooke
Clse

Oxbottom
Close

Bannisters Field

Blind   Lane

Ketches

Beechland

Challey Lane

artom

Church Road

Church Rd

Broomlye

Gipp's
Wood

Markstakes Lane

Ridgeland
Farm

Hotel
Newick
Park

Mackerel's

Rocks

Gipp's
Farm

Sutton
Hall

Tufts Farm

F G H 261 J K

High
House Farm

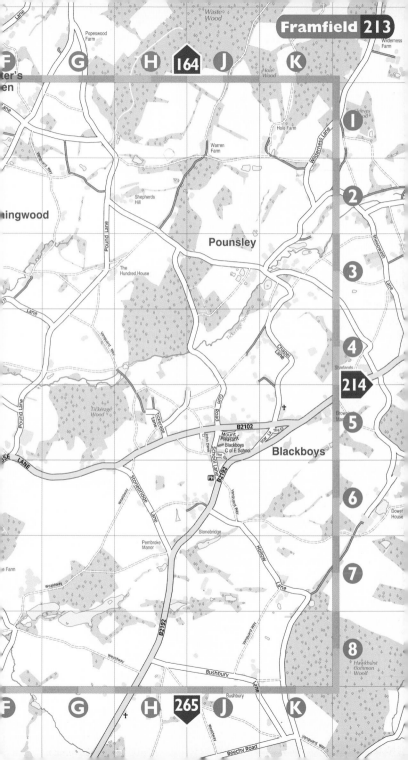

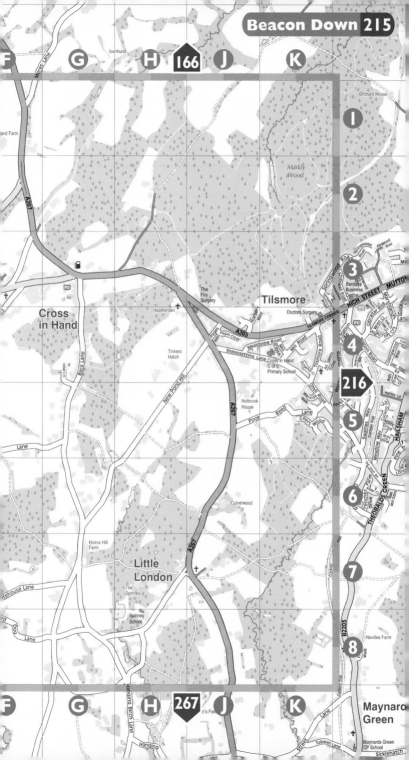

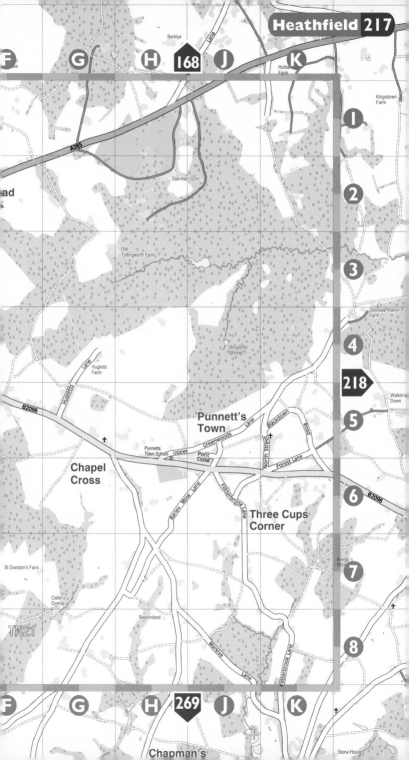

F   G   H   **170**   J   K

Green Farm

Park Farm

Bowman's
Farm

Kemland

High
Wood

Berryman's
Farm

River Darkwell

llingford Farm

Perch
Hill Farm

Rounden
Wood

ttle
orge Farm

Great
Worge

220

tling
rk

Brighting
Down

Carrick's
Hill

Christmas
Farm

Turner's
Farm

B2096

B2096

Wood's Corner

Dallington
School

Haselden Farm

Dallington

Lane

ourn

F   G   H   **271**   J   K

High
Wood

Haselden
Wood

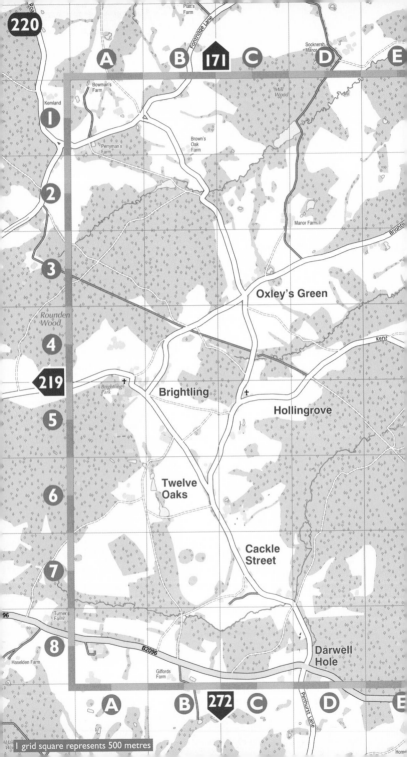

F G H **172** J K

1

2

3

4

222

5

Mountfie

6

7

8

F G H **273** J K

1

Newhouse
Farm

Brightling
Hall

Scalands
Farm

Peans

Darvell

Brown's
Farm

Scalands
Wood

Glottenham Stream

Glottenham
Manor

Mountfield Park
Farm

Park
Pale

Mountfield Lane

Darwell
Reservoir

Tunstall
Farm

Taylor's
Cottage

Baldwin's
Farm

The
Banks

Castle Farm

Crowhurst Wood

Crowhurst
Farm

Down

Oxley's
Down

Neth
Primary School

Netherfield
Court

Netherfield
Way

Netherfield

Netherfield Road

Eatenden Lane

Eatenden Wood

1 grid square represents 500 metres

A B **175** C D E

I

Staplecross
School

Staplecross

Weald View
Mill
Sheriffland
Forge
Lane
Cricketers
Field
B2165
†

Staplecross

**Collier's
Green**

B2165

Lordine
Court

Martins
Farm

Sandersons Lane

2

The Grange

Gate
Farm

Sparks

3

Beacon Lane

The
Beacon

Ellenwhorne

Stockwood
Farm

Ellenwhorne Lane

Cripp's
Corn

223

Miles
Farm

Stocklands
Farm

Ellenwhorne Lane

4

Compasses

B2244

B2244
Junction Road

Catts
Green Farm

B2089

5

Streetfield
Wood

Brede High
Wood

6

Beech
Farm
House

Beech Farm Road

7

Powdermill
Reservoir

Hurst Lane

Hurst Wood

8

Churchland Lane

Hurst House

Jacob's
Farm

A B **276** C D E

Hurst Lane

Brede Lane

High

F
G
H **176**
J
K

Watts Hill
Farm

Adams Lane

New Road

Dodsell
Lane

Sherbourne
Valley

A28

B2165

I

Commons
Wood Farm

Morley
Farm

2

Great Stent
Farm

St Palace Lane

New
House
Farm

B2165

Horns
Cross

Tanhouse
Farm

✝

✝ Doucegrove

3

4

NORTHIAM

Maplestone
Farm

Conster
Manor

226

Chitcombe

Brede High
Green

ROAD

5

Furnace Lane

Hop's Close

Broad
Oak

6

Goatham
Green

CHITCOMBE

Powdermill La

Goatham

Lane

ROAD

The Hawkhurst Rd
Gatehurst

Farm
Drive

Cashin
Drive

Chestnut

Broad Cl

Beaufort Rd

Fieldway

Doctors
Surgery

UDIMOR

7

D

Powdermill Lane

Moorsholm

WOOD HILL

✝ Brede County
Primary
School

B20

Reyson Oasts

8

KING ST

A28

CACKLE STREET

F
G
H **277**
J
K

Conster Street

Mary
Close

Pottery Lane

St Lane

Steep Hill Brede Lane

Pottery

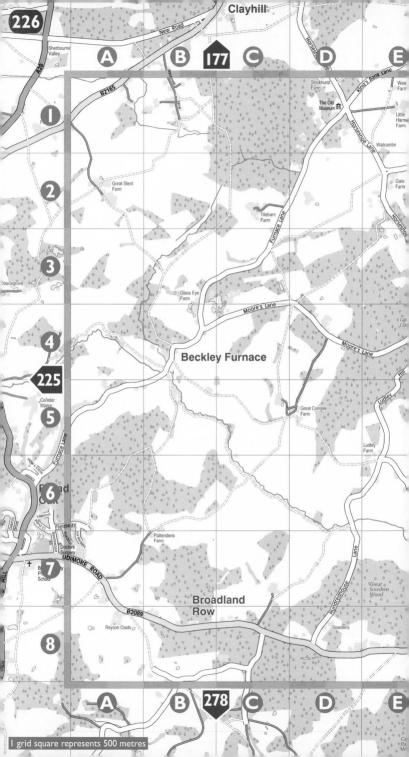

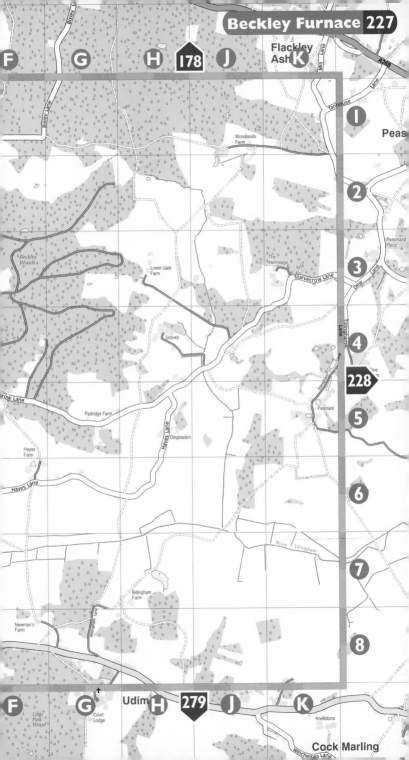

F G H **178** J **Flackley Ash** K

I

Peas

2

Peasmarsh Place

3

4

228

5

6

7

8

F G **Udim** H **279** J K

Bixley Lane

A268

Mill Lane

Tanhouse Lane

Woodlands Farm

Beckley Woods

Lower Gate Farm

The Hermitage

Starvecrow Lane

Dew Lane

Tillingham Lane

Pelsham

Groves

Hayes Lane

Dinglesden

row Lane

Partridge Farm

Hayes Lane

Hayes Farm

River Tillingham

Billingham Farm

Newman's Farm

Billingham Lane

Little Park Wood

Court Lodge

Knellstone

Cock Marling

Winchelsea Lane

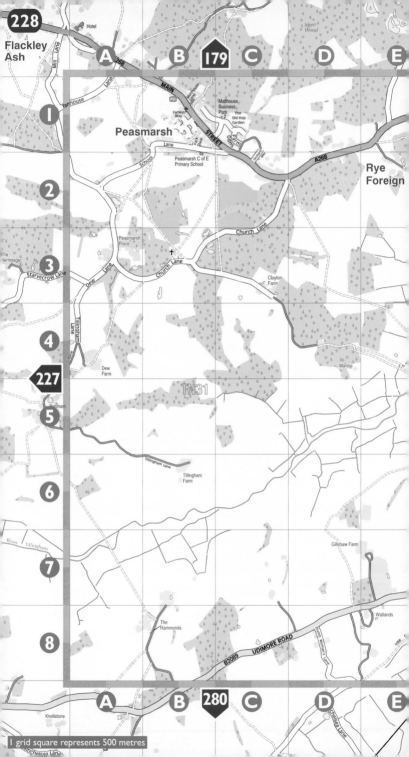

F8
1 New Lydd Rd

F G H J K

I

2

3

Little Cheyne
Court

4

232

5

6

7

8
...omhill Level

Kent Ditch

Barn Farm

Kent County
East Sussex County

Camber

Farm Lane

Draffin Lane

New Lydd Road

Old Lydd Road

Guldeford
Lane Corner

GULDEFOR...

F G H 283 J K

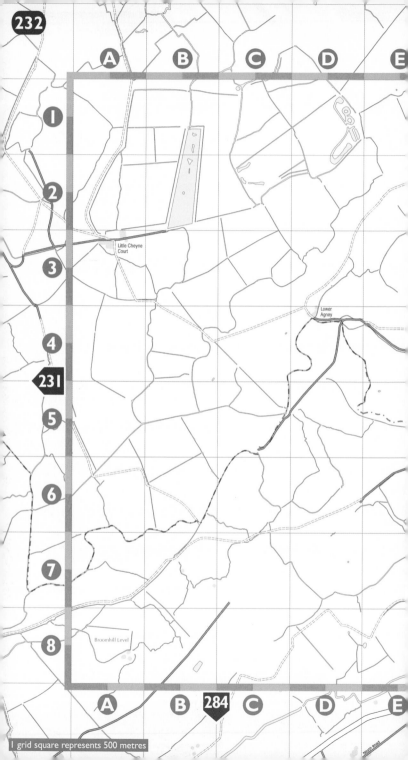

232

A   B   C   D   E

1

2

3   Little Cheyne
     Court

Lower
Agney

4

231

5

6

7

8   Broomhill Level

A   B   284   C   D   E

1 grid square represents 500 metres

F
G
H
J
K

I

2

3

4

5

6

7

8

Hawk Corner

Newland Farm

Newland

Little Scotney

Kent County
East Sussex County

Pigwell

Duty's Gap Road

Gap Road

Scotney Court

West Ripe

LC
LC
LC

The Forelands

F
G
H
J
K

Heath Road
Ferguson Road

Stone

Ferguson Road

LC

South Brooks Road

LC

Invicta Road

H Bones Farm

Swa

234

A B 182 C D E

Coulters
Dean Fm

Head
Down Plantation

1

Queen
Elizabeth
Forest

2

Oakham
Bottom

Downley

Newbarn Road

3

Ditcham
Park Sch

4

Glass
Brow

Sussex

5

Sussex Border Path

6 Farm
on Lane

Chalton PH

Woodcroft
Fm

Harris La.

7

Sussex Border Path

South Lane

8

South Lane

Sussex Border Path

A B 287 C D E

1 grid square represents 500 metres

F   G   H   **183**   J   K

I
2
3
4
236
5
6
7
8

Forty Acre Lane

Sunwood Fm

South Downs Way

Leith Copse

Cow

B2146

South Downs Way

Sussex Border Path

Foxcombe Fm

West Harting Down

Round Down

NT Uppark

B2146

Sussex Border Path

Hale Wood

Eckensfield

Hucksholt Fm

B2146

Little Green School

Cowdown Lane

Cowdown Fm

F   G   H   **288**   J   K

Compton

School Lane

Compton & Upmarden C of E Primary School

B2146

240

Cocking Park

A **B** **188** **C** Oatscroft **D** **E**

Dunford

Bex Lane

Heyshott Green

Mill Lane

Peace Rd

1

Hoe Copse

2

Heyshott

The Cross

High Meadow

Down Close

3

Cocking

PO Mill La

Church La

Ma

4

239

5

Lane Barn

Heyshott Down

Manorfarm Down

South Downs Way

South Downs Way

6

7

Charlton Forest

olverstone Farm

Herringdean Wood

8

Singleton Forest

A **B** **293** **C** **D** **E**

Broadham House

Wood Lease

I grid square represents 500 metres

Graffham Common

F G H 189 J K

Topleigh

Hoyle Farm

Shrublands

Wiblings Farm

Hoyle

I

2

Nonnington La

3

Woodcote Farm

Graffham

P.O

4

Calloways

Hayland Farm

242

Tagents Farm

Downlands School

5

6

Broad Walk

Tegleaze Farm

7

Tegleaze

Eastdean Wood

Lamb Leg

8

F G H 294 J K

North Side

A

B

190

C

D

E

Graffham
Common

Barnett's Farm

Lavington
Common

Shrublands

1 Willings Farm

Northwood Farm

Westerlands
Stud

2

Nonnington
La

**Upper
Norwood**

3

Norwood Lane

Old Park

Graffham

4

Calloways

Lavington Stud Farm

5 Downlands
School

The Drive

**East
Lavington**

Norwood Lane North

6

Norwood La
South

Sealord
College

Beechwood

Woolavington
Down

7 Tegleaze Farm

Tegleaze

South Downs Way

8

A

B

Dun

295

255

C

D

E

244

A   B   192   C   D   E

1

2

Burton Park Road

Burton Mill Pond

3

Crouch Farm

4

243

5

Sutton End

6

7

Sutton

8

PH

Greenfield

River Rother

Shopham Bridge

Bigenor Farm

Coates

Coates Castle

Coa

Coates Lane

Broad Halfpenny

Bignor Park Cott

Bignor Park Road

Bignor

Bignorpark

School Lane

Hadworth Farm

A   B   297   C   D   E

I grid square represents 500 metres

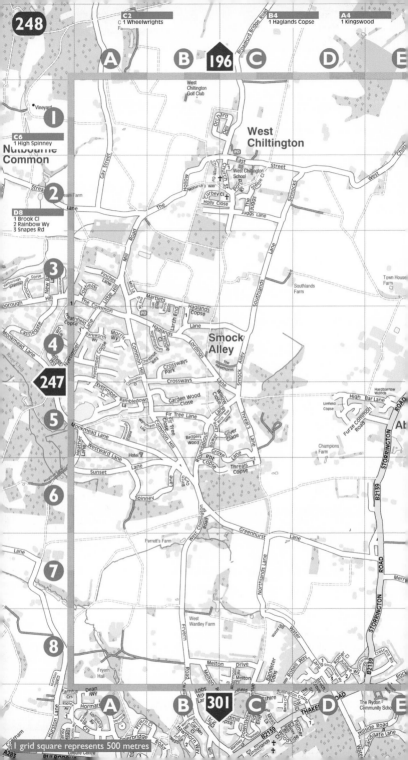

Wyndham
Farm

Winenham Lane

Gratten Lane

Abbeylands
Farm

A

B

C

Great
Wapses
Farm

D

Gratten Lane

E

I

Fieldlands
Farm

Lane

2

Sm Lane

Lanehurst

3

Morley Farm

Firsland Farm

Firsland
Park
Estate

Heatenthorn
Farm

Park Farm

4

Blackstone Gate
Farm

B2116

High
Cross

5

Kingsfold

Trusler's
Hill Farm

Trusler's Hill

Woodhouse

6

Bylsborough
Farm

Blackstone Lane

Lane

7

Blackstone St

Blackstone

8

Woodmancote
Place

Wick
Farm

A

B

C

D

E

Woodmancote

Terry's
Cross

Shives Wood

A2

1 grid square represents 500 metres

205

258

310

KEYMER

Ditchling

G5
1 The Paddocks

G6
1 Station Cl

F
G
H
207
J
K

Bower Farm

I

H6
1 South Downs

2

Southam

Heath
Farm

*Great
Home
Wood*

Shaw
Park

3

Inholms Farm

Honeypot

Lane

4

Chapel
Rd

WOODGATE
VIEW

Homewoodgate
Farm

Shepherns Way

260

Yokehurst

5

Wells
Cl

West
Gate

Plumpton Green

North Barnes
Farm

North
Hall

Riddens
Lane

Riddens
La

Rudgling Rd

Plumpton New
Primary
School

North
Barnes
Lane

East Pk
Fields

LC

Barnfield

LC

6

Plumpton Station

Plumpton
Race Course

Plumpton
Lane

Rylands

Mount
Pleasant

Novington Lane

Highbridge Lane

7

Brookhouse

Chiltington L

Ashurst

**East
Chiltington**

Chapel Lane

LC

8

Lane

PH

Woolton Farm

The Old
Mill Ho

F
G
H
312
J
K

Chilt

A   B   208   C   D   E

C4
1 Appledene Cnr
2 Grantham Cl
3 Green La
4 Hornbuckles Cl

B4
1 Whitegates Cl

Chailey

Ades

Wild
Woo

The
Hooke

1

Markstakes
Farm

Markstakes   Lane

Southam

South
Street

2

Markstakes
Common

Caveridge   Lane

3

South
Common

St John Bank

Lane

Honey

Lane

Chailey
Comprehensive
School

Woodworks Lane

South Chailey

Balneath
Manor

4

259

Shepherds Way

Bouchands Drive

Yokehurst

Old Barns
Farm

5

North
Hall

Woodbrooks
Farm

6

Mount
Pleasant

Highbridge   Lane

Hurst
Barns

Hewenstreet
Farm

7

Novington

Chiltington   Lane

LC

RESTING OAK HL

Wootton Farm

8

Chiltington

A   B   313   C   Win   arm   D   E

RESTING O

1 grid square represents 500 metres

262

Mackerel's Rocks

Vuggles Farm

Gipp's

A **B** **210** **C** **D** **E**

Constantia Manor

New House Farm

Gipp's Wood

Sutton Hall

1

Longford Stream

2

Beaks Farm

Longford Farm

River Ouse

Station Road

Tile Barn Cl

Isfield

3

Spithurst

PO

4

Burtenshaw Farm

261

Mount Pleasa

5

Anchor Lane

Collins Lane

Scufflings

Delves Farm

Boathouse Farm

Lewes Road

Lane

6

Banks Farm

7

PH

Oakl Park

Kiln

xfield Road

8

Crink Hill

Iron River

Barcombe Mills Road

Barcombe House

Upper Clay Hill Farm

A **B** **315** **C** **D** **E**

1 grid square represents 500 metres

Mou
Eph

F G H 211 J K

Ridgewood
House

Horstedpond
Farm

Ridgewood Stream

New

I

2

A22

Hotel

Horsted
Place

Little
Horsted
School

Little
Horsted

Worth
Farm

River Uck

East Sussex
National
Golf Club

3

Bradford's
Farm

Wicklands

Lane

4

264

Old
Farm

Brockwells
Farm

5

A26

Crump's
Wood

se

Plashett
Park

6

Moatpark
Farm

Cooper's
Hatch

7

Plashett
Wood

Mount Farm

Harvey's Lane

8

F G H 316 J K

Red
Barn Farm

Upper
Lodge Farm

F   G   H   **213**   J   K

B2192

Vanguard Way

Westway

Bushbury Lane

Bushbury

I

Beechy Road

Squires Farm
Industrial
Estate

**Eason's
Green**

B2192

**Hawkhurst
Common**

Beechy Road

Vanguard Way

2

Hope Farm

3

J6
1 Carpenters Cft

Pilgrim Hall

Westway

Firgrove

**Davis's
Town**

Barham House

4

266

Bentley
Wood

Old
Whyly

Belmont

5

London Road

Thomas Turner Drive

Waldron Road

Mill Lane

**East
Hoathly**

6

Susans
Close

East Hoathly
C of E School

High Street

Buttsfield Lane

Ruxbyte

Kings Lane

The
Mews

East
Hoathly
Surgery

Westway

Halland Park Farm

South Street

7

Rowland
Wood

A22

8

F   G   H   **318**   J   K

Harr
Corner

Price's
Farm

Lane

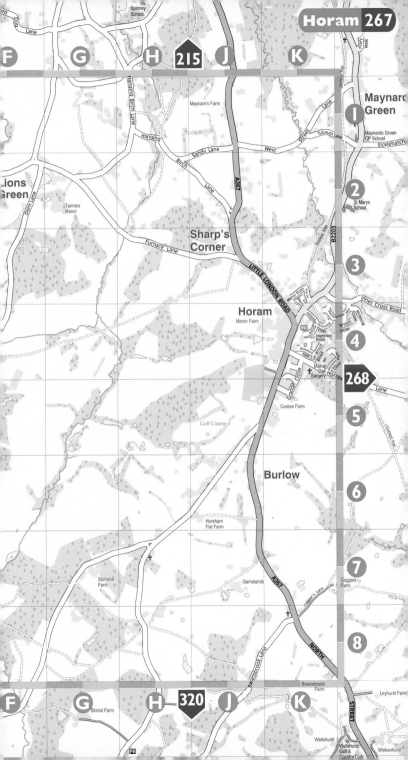

TN21

Beaconland

F **G** **H** **217** **J** **K**

MARLEY LANE

Fitteworth Lane

I

Stone House

Chapman's Town

Rushlake Green

PH

2 Great Iwood

Warbleton

PH

Hammer Lane

Kingsley Hill Farm

Back Lane

3

Bathurst Farm

4

Tilement Farm

270

Iwood Place Farm

5

Durrants Farm

Beech Hill Farm

6

Egynt Farm

Cralle Place

7

Hammer Lane

Foul Mile

Furnace Brook

8

Court Horeham

F **G** **H** **322** **J** **K**

Bemzells Lane

Hammer Lane

Trolliloes

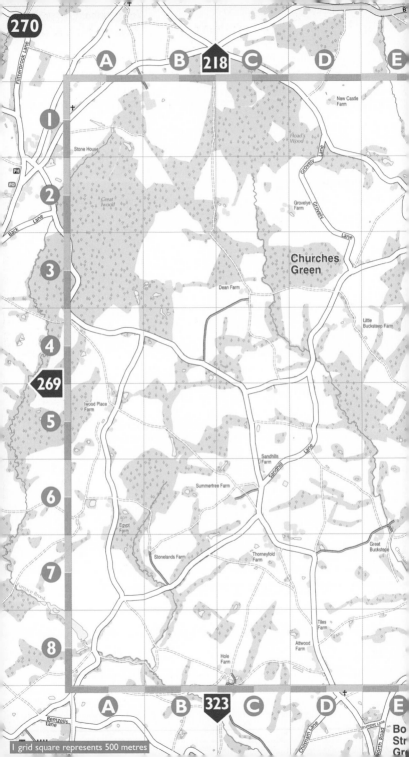

Wood's Corner

F Dallington **G** **H** **219** **J** **K** Haselden

I

2

3

272

4

5

6

7

8

Brownbread Street

F **G** **H** **324** **J** **K**

High Wood

Haselden Wood

Pannelridge Wood

B2096

B2096

Turner's

Dallington School

Herrings Farm

Padgham Down Farm

Silverick's Lane

Silvericks Farm

Buckwell Farm

Thornden Farm

Lattenden Farm

Woodlands Farm

le Farm

steep or

Glyde's Farm

Pear Tree Farm

Brigden Hill Farm

Court Lodge

New Buildings Farm

Ponts Green

1066 Country Walk

South Lane

Herring's Road

Lattenhurst Lane

Lattenhurst Lane

Farthing Lane

Lane

Ashhurst Fields

's Gill

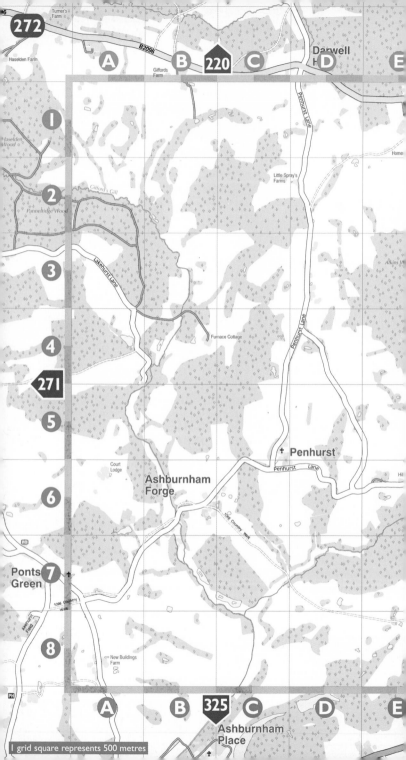

Turner's Farm

B2096

Haselden Farm

A

Giffords Farm

B

C

Darwell

D

E

I

Haselden Wood

Penhurst Lane

2

Gifford's Gill

Pannelridge Wood

Little Spray's Farms

3

Lakehurst Lane

Atkins V

4

Furnace Cottage

Penhurst Lane

5

Penhurst

6

Court Lodge

Ashburnham Forge

Penhurst Lane

Hill

Ponts Green

7

The Country Walk

1096 Country Walk

8

New Buildings Farm

PH

A

B

C

D

E

Ashburnham Place

I grid square represents 500 metres

D6
1 Abbey Wy
2 Rue De Bayeux

D5
1 The Cloisters

B7
1 Highgrove

Crowhurst

A
B
222
C
D
E

1
Eatenden Lane
Eatenden Wood
Wood's Place
Woodsdale

2
Burnthouse Wood

3
Canadia
Le Rette Farm
Lower Gate Farm

Netherfield Hill

Canadia Road

Whatlington Road

4
Kingswell Farm

273
5
Ashes Wood
Beech Farm

Wattle's Wish

Netherfield Road

Virgin's Lane
Brown's Drive
Dukes Rd
Uckham Lan

Caldbec Hill

BATTLE

6
Rother District Council

Chain Lane

Caldbec Hill

Littl

Mount Joy

7
A271 NORTH TRADE ROAD
Battle Hospital
Claverham Community College

Battle Gate's
Hampden Close
Asten Flds

Battle & Langton School

Martins Oak Surgery
Doctors Surgery
Battle Museum

Park Lane
Battle Abbey School

UPPER LAKE

8
Tower Hill

POWDERMILL LANE

Great Park Farm

TN33

A
B
327
C
D
E

B2095

Hotel

F G H 227 J K

J5
New Farm 1 High Fords Cl

K5
1 Peartree Fld

Udimore

Court Lodge

Little Park Wood

Knellstone

I

K6
1 Oast House Rd
2 Tithe Barn Fld

Cock M

Winchelsea Lane

2

Float Farm

3

4

280

5

Brook Farm

1066 Country Walk

Broad Street

Icklesham

Parsonage Lane

PH

Icklesham Primary School

Oast House Fld

Broad Street

Toke Farm

Brede Valley View

High Fords Cl

PO

Manor Cl

Manor Farm

Workhouse Lane

+

6

1066 Country Walk

A259(T) MAIN ROAD

Laurel Lane

Watermill Lane

Main Road

Roughters

7

Scrag Oak

Knockbridge Farm

Pannel Sewer

8

Pannel Farm

Pickham Farm

Pannel

F G H 332 J K

A   B   230   C   D   E

Rye
Harbour

Rye Harbour
Sailing Club

Coastguard

Train Road

1

2

Nook
Beach

3

Watch
House

4

281

5

Nature
Reserve

Rye Golf
Club

Poin

Simpsons
Industrial
Estate

6

7

8

A   B   C   D   E

1 grid square represents 500 metres

G1
1 Peter James Cl
2 Tonbridge Wy

J1
1 Saunders Wy

Drama Lane

New Lydd Road

Old Lydd Road

Tanyard Way

Watery Lane

Martello Drive

Tonham Way

PO First Avenue

Second Avenue

The Suttons

Lydd Road

Broomhill Farm

Broomhill Level

Combe

231

ve Bay

nds

F G H J K

F G H J K

I
2
3
4
284
5
6
7
8

A   B   232   C   D   E

I

Broomhill Level

Broomhill Farm

2

Jury's
Gap

Lydd Road

Neath Road

Neath Road

M

Broomhill Sands

3

4

283

5

6

7

8

A   B   C   D   E

I grid square represents 500 metres

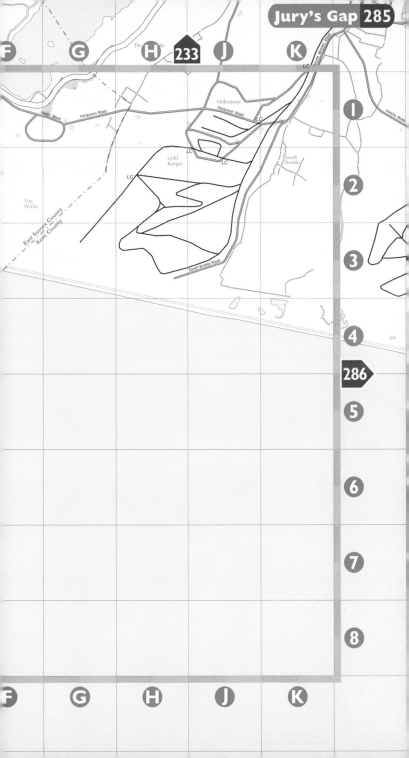

F G H 233 J K

South Brooks Road

LC

I

Invicta Road

Heath Road   Ferguson Road

Holmstone

Ferguson Road

LC

LC

LC

Lydd
Ranges

South
Brooks

LC

2

The
Wicks

East Sussex County
Kent County

3

South Brooks Road

4

286

5

6

7

8

F G H J K

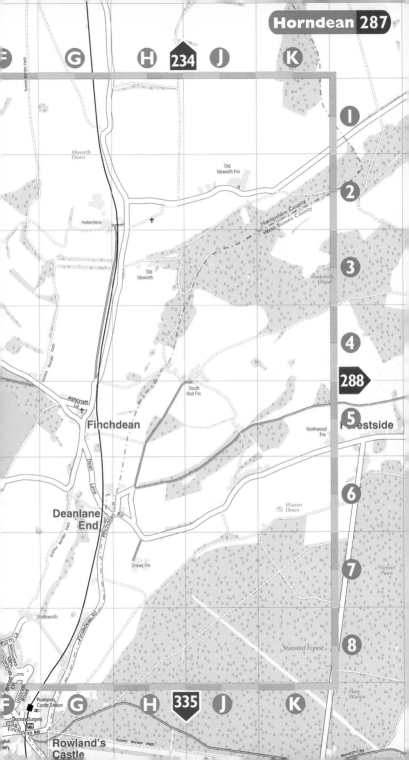

F G H 234 J K

1
2
3
4
288
5
6
7
8

Idsworth Down

Old Idsworth Fm

Heberdens

Hampshire County
West Sussex County

Old Idsworth

Markwells Wood

South Holt Fm

Ashcroft La

Finchdean

Northwood Fm

Forestside

Deanlane End

Warren Down

Drews Fm

Wellsworth

Stansted Forest

Flint Piece

Flare Warren

F G H 335 J K

Rowlands
Castle Station

Doctors Surgery
PO
PH
Finchdean Rd

**Rowland's
Castle**

Sussex Border Path

Monarch's Way

288

A　B　235　C　D　E

1

Compton

School Lane
ⓘ
Compton &
Upmarden C of
Primary School

2

Hampshire County
West Sussex County

3

Markwells
Wood

Horsley Farm

Locksash Lane

West Marden

4

Nore
Down

287

Elton Down Wy

Oldhouse
Lane

B2146

5

Northwood
Fm

Forestside

Lodge Fm

Lodge Lane

6

Warren
Down

7

Firtree
Piece

Broadreed Fm

8

Stansted

Lumley Seat

A　B　336　C　D　E

Monarch's Wy

Woodlands

Woodlands
Cotts

F
G
H 236
J
K

I

East Mard

2

3

4

290

5

6

7

Stoughton

8

Bevis's Thumb

Long Lane

Long Lane

Up Marden

ocksash Fm

Grevitts Copse

Lowerfarm Copse

Locksash Lane

Haslett Copse

Inholmes Wood

Pitlands Fm

Monarch's Way

Church Farm

B2146

E
G
H 337
J
K

Monarch's Way

Monarch's Way

COOKS Lane

Walderton

290

Lane

A   B   237   C   D   E

1

+
East
Marden

East
Marden
Down

Hillbarn

2

Phillinwood La
B2141

3

Wildhams
Wood

4

289

5

Inholmes
Wood

6

Stoughton
Down

Monarch's Way

7

Monarch's Way

+
Church
Farm

Stoughton

8

A   B   338   C   D   E

I grid square represents 500 metres

F G H **238** J K

Staple
Ash Farm

Colworth
Down

I

ve

2 Farm

Kyte's Lane

3

Hylters

Monarch's Way

Monarch's Way

Lodge
Hill Farm

4

292

West Dea
Gardens

Heathbarn
Down

5 Way

Monarch's Way

Brickkiln Farm

West Dean C of E
Primary School

Church

6

Hasler's

Lane

A286

7

Preston
Farm

8 018

B2141

Crows Hall Farm

Binderton Lane

F G H **339** J K

F G H 240 J K

I

2

3

4

294

5

6

7

8

Broadham House

Yorkhurst Hill

North Lane

Wood Lease

North Down

ewhouse Farm

170
Levin Down
Nature Reserve

rhouse Lane

New

Road

PH

Charlton Road

PO

Chapel Row

Charlton

East
Dean

Main Road

PH

Monarch's Way

Eastdean Hill

Eastdean
Park

Monarch's Way

Goodwood
Country
Park

Selhurstpark Road

Pilleygreen Lodges

Clay

Charlton
Park

Road

Charlton
Down

Goodwood
Race Course

Monarch's Way

Open
Winkins

Eastdean Hill

F G H 341 J K

Hill Dr
Monarch's Way
Park Rd

Motcombe Broadwalk

F G H **242** J K

Dogkennel Cottages

I

255
Duncton Hill

Littleton Farm

2

A285

South Downs Way

†

Upwaltham

3

Droke Lane

West Wood

4

296

5

Benges Wood

6

North Wood

7

Eartham Wood

8

A285

Dogkennel Cottages

A B **243** C D E

Greenfiel

I

Folly Lane

Glatting Lane

2

Glatting Farm

South Downs Way

3

Coldharbour Farm

4

West

Glatting Lane South Downs Way

◄**295**

Burton Down

South Downs Way

5

Monarch's Way

6

Monarch's Way

Great Bottom

Gumber Farm

7

Stammers

8

A B **344** C D E

F G H 244 J K

I

2

3

4

298

5

6

7

8

Bury
Mill Farm

A29

ROAD

Bignor

Hadworth Farm

West Burton Lane

West
Burton

W Burton Lane

225
Bignor Hill

West

Burton

Bury School
Lane

BURY HILL

South Downs Way

Coombe
Wood

South Downs Way

South Downs Way

South Downs Way

The Denture

Houghton
Forest

A29

Monarch's Way

Monarch's Way

B2139

F G H 345 J K

Parlets Farm

Whiteways
Lodge

A29 A284

F G H **246** J K

I

2

3

4

300

5

6

7

8

F G H **347** J K

Greatham
Common

Amberley Wild Brooks

Rackham
Street

Rackham

Rackham   Street

Cross
Gate

Rackham   Road

East Street

Arun
Hurst   Cottage
Hurst

Amberley

Amberley School

TURNPIKE ROAD

B2139

Parham
Historic
House

Mill

south Downs Way

South Downs Way

Downs
Farm

The Burgh

F1
1 Holly Ct
2 Shermanbury Dr

F2
1 Holly Cl

G Melton Driv **H** Bannister Gdns **248** **J** **K** Road

I

G1
1 Frenches
2 Riverside

2

G2
1 Brewers Yd
2 Chanctonb'y Wk
3 Manor Cl
4 Mant Cl
5 Rectory Rd
6 Rectory Wk
7 Rosemary Cl

3 STORRIN

H2
1 Chantry Cl
2 Wisborough La

4

302

5

J1
1 Heatherlands

6

K1
1 Hillside Wk

7

8

Sullington
Warren

Sullington

The Rydon
Community School

Hillside Road

Sandgate Lane

Abbots
Leigh

WASHINGTON R

Barns Farm

Gerston
Business
Park

Greyfriars

The Chantry

Chantry Lane

South Downs Way

South Downs Way

Cobden
Farm

F **G** **H** **349** **J** **K**

West Street
HIGH ST
SCHOOL HILL
MANLEY'S HILL
A283
THAKEHAM ROAD
B2139
B2139
North Street
The Glebe
Surgery
School Lane
Storrington
Lawn Tennis
Club
Ravenscroft Wy
Post
Gal
Meadowside
Brown's Lane
Storrington

STORRINGTON

F G H 254 J K

I

Wick Farm

Shaves Farm

Shaves Wood

Woodmancote

Terry's Cross

2

A281

Bramlands Lane

Bramlands

Holmbush Farm

Holmbush Lane

3

Catsland Lane

Catsland Lane

tsland m

Edburton Drove

4

Clappers Lane

Badger Wood Farm

rynings ne Farm

308

urton Barn

5

Perching Sands Farm

Drove

Edburton

Brook House

6

Poy

Perching Drove

Drove

7

Wickhurst Barns

urton

†

Fulking

Perching Manor Farm

Stammers Hill

†

8

South Downs Way

Devil's Dyke Road

F G H 355 J K

308

A   B **255** C   D   E

BRIGHTON

Muddleswood
Brighton Rd
B2117

1

Shaves Farm

Shaves Wood

Locks Green Farm

London Road

Randolph's Copse

2

Park Wood

LONDON ROAD

3

A281

Church Lane

4

307

Poynings Grange Farm

WEST   ROAD   A281

Rest Farm

5

Brook House

6

Mill Cl
Mill La

The Good Start School

Beggar's Lane

Manor Farm Business Centre

Poynings

PH

7

Wickhurst Barns

Saddlescombe

8

Devil's Dyke

A   B **356** C   D   E

South Downs Way

Way

1 grid square represents 500 metres

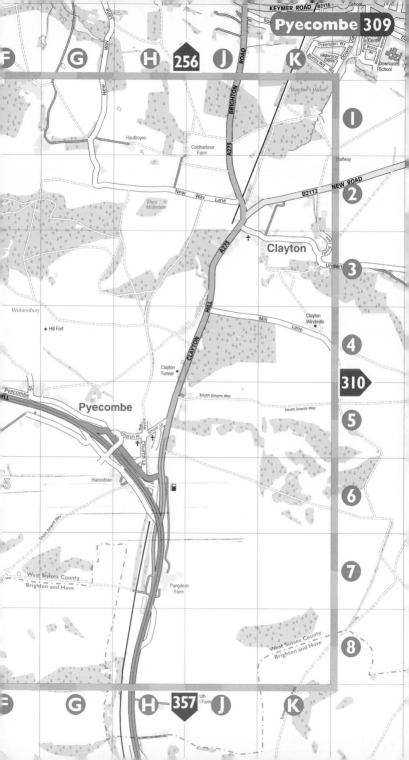

Streat

Nodes

F   G   H   **258**   J   K

I

ES

ROAD

B2116

Sedlow Wood

Bricks Wood

Street Lane

2

Middleton Manor

3

Wards Farm

Westmeston

The Gate

B2116

4

Street Bostal

312

Plumpton

South Downs Way

5

Streathill Farm

6

7

Park

8

Stanmer Down

F   G   H   **359**   J   K

St Mary's Farm

Chiltington

312

259

A B C D E

Ashurst

Neth

Old Ho

Chapel Lane

PH

1

Stantons Farm

Street Lane

2

Plumpton Lane

Novington Manor

Novington Lane

3

Wales Farm

Warningore Farm

4

B2116

Plumpton

Novington Farm

311

5

Plumpton Bostall

South Downs Way

Plumpton Plain

Blackcap

eathill m

6

7

South Downs Way

Asbcombe Bottom

8

Buckland Bank

South Downs Way

A B C D E

360

Balmer Down

I grid square represents 500 metres

261

C8
1 Bridgewick Cl
2 Fitzgerald Rd
3 Lambert Pl
4 Malling Cl
5 The Martlets

B8
1 Hoopers Cl
2 Mealla Cl
3 Peckham Cl

Deadmantree Hill

Shelley's Folly

PESTING OAK HILL A275

Conyboro

Mill Lane

Church Road

Barcombe

Culver Farm

Averys

I

2

3 Cooksbridge

Cooksbridge Station

School

Chandler's Mead

Hamsey Lane

North End

Cowlease Farm

4

313

5

Hamsey House

Winterton Lane

Hamsey

Chalkham Farm

Ivors Lane

Offham

The Drove

6

Hamseyplace Farm

6

7

Lower Stoneham

Stoneham Farms

Upper Stoneham

7

A275

River Ouse

Mantell Close

Monks Way

Durovan Close

Old Malling Farm

Old Malling Way

Bexhurst

The Mount

A26

MALLING DOWN

8

Churchill Road

Landport

Stoneham

Bouquet Cl

Godfrey Cl

Malling

Queen's Rd

South Malling Primary School

Mill Rd

MALLING STREET

The Chets

A2029

Lewes Wallands CP School

Highdown Road

OFFHAM ROAD

A27

Meridian Rd

Pells C of E Infant School

LEWES

Lewes Business Centre

Riverside Industrial Est

Phoenix Industrial Estate

St Michael's Sports Grnd

Hereward Way

Spences

Primary School

Sussex Rd

Southdown Business Park

Downs Primary School

The Spinneys

Wheatsheaf Gardens

BROOKS ROAD

Davey's La

A26

D

E

1 grid square represents 500 metres

265

A   B   C   D   E

Laughton
Park Farm

1

Walls Farm

Park Corner

Price's Farm

2

Upper Vert Wood

3

Brickhurst Farm

Lower Vert Wood

Laughton

4

317

5

County Primary School

B2124

B2124

Stone Cross Farm

Broomham

B2124

Broomham Farm

6

Marchants Farm

Milward's Farm

Church Lane

7

Cleaver's Farm

8

A   B   C   D   E

366

Mark Cross

1 grid square represents 500 metres

F G H J K

266

I
2
3
4

320

5
6
7
8

Hilder's Court

Stream

Highlands Farm
Frith's Farm

Wealdway

Parsonage Farm

Vanguard Way

Chiddingly Place

Hale Green

Chiddingly

PH

PO

Chiddingly Cricket Club

Wealdway

Wealdway

Little Park Farm

Hamly Bridge

Scraper's Hill

water's end

Chiddingly CP School

Muddles Green

Thunder's Hill

House

Vanguard Way

Burgh Hill

Holmes's Hill

PO

Golden Cross

PO

A22

Nash Street

Hackhurst Stud

The Old Farmhouse

Northfield Business Park

Hackhurst Lane

A22

L
D

Camberlot Hall

Camberlot Road

Vanguard Way

Limekiln Farm

Field House

F G H J K

367

Clover Farm

320

267

A **B** **C** **D** **E**

Stream
Mill

1

Hale
Green

Strood Farm

PH

Gun
Hill

Weatheway

Swanbrook Lane

2

West
Street Farm

Weatheway

3

Hamly Bridge

Hill

World's
End
Farm

4

319

Pekes House

Hill

5

Perryland Farm

Broad Farm

Granary
Business
Centre

6

Hackhurst
Stud

Lane

Hackhurst Lane

Camberlot Lane

NORTH STREET B2104

7

Northfield Business
Park

A22

Lower
Dicker

Lower
Horsebridge

A271

A267

8

Carr Road

Camberlot
Hall

Hatches
Farm

Camberlot Road

Knight's Farm

Hotel

Upper Horseb

A **B** **C** **D** **E**

d House

368

Starnash

F8
1 Old Mill Cl

G8
1 Beckenham Cl
2 Hawkstown Cl
3 Hawkstown Gdns

F **G** **H** 268 **J** **K**

Goldbridge Farm
Knightsbr
Court
Horeham

I

H8
1 Pembroke Cl
2 Warwick Cl

Leyhurst Farm

Grove
Park

Grove Hill

Grove Hill

2
Blackford Farm

Winkenhurst

Cinderford Lane

Fontmills

3

Holmbush

Springham Farm

Jarvis's
Wood

Blackstock Farm

4

STREET

Grove Hill

322 ▶

Shawpits Farm

5

Tanyard Lane

Amberstone
Hospital

Hellingly Hospital

Park Wood

6
Carter's Corner
Place

Station Road

Mill Lane

Grove Hill

New Road

Amberstone
Hospital

7

Magham
Down

Park Road

Park Farm

AMBERSTONE

8

A271

Amberstone
Grange Farm

UPPER HORSEBRIDGE ROAD

HAWKSWOOD ROAD

Danum
Close

Ashley Gardens

BN27

Quintin
Medical Centre

A271

Hawkus
Farm CP
School

A295

F **G** **H** 369 **J** **K**

Leap Cross
Small
Business Centre

Harthylands Crescent

Oak Tree
Way

F G H 270 J K

1
2
3
4
324
5
6
7
8

Tiles Farm
Attwood Farm
Hole Farm

Chilsham Lane

Humpet Lane

North Road

Bodle Street Green

Beard's Farm

Ale House Farm

Prinkle Lane

Prinkle Farm

Cowden Farm

Chilsham

Nunningham Farm

Lane

Bagham Lane

James Avenue
Fairfield
Monceux West
Terrace
Monceux Road
West End
Tanyard
The Acre
Bell Road
Herstmonceux
The Surgery
Herstmonceux C of E School

GARDNER STREET

CHILSHAM ROAD

A271

Victoria Rd
Coombe
Dale
Circle
Hurst Lane
Highview Cl
The Surgery
Nursery Lane
Joe's Lane

Windmill Hill

PO

Lime Park

Chapel Row

A271

Win Hill

Tiley Lane

Flowers Green

Butler's Lane

Comphurst

Comphurst Lane

Wartling Road

Herstmonceux Place

Golden Cross

Lower

Church

Cherry Croft Farm

Wartling Wood

Cham

F G H 371 J K

F G H 272 J K

Ashburnham Place

A271

Agmerhurst Farm

Burnt Barns Farm

1

2

3

Coombe Hill Farm

Marlpits Lane

4

326

5

Ninfield

A271

A269

Standard Hill Cl

Combe La

Manchester Road

The Surgery

HIGH STREET

The Green

THE GREEN

Bexhill Rd

A269

Downs Vw

Ninfield C E School

A269

Hazard's Green

Standard Hill House

Moor Hill Drive

6

Lower Street

B2095

7

A269

Wet Wood

R STREET

Crouch

Lane

WODE ROAD

8

Russell's Green

Pashley Farm

F G H 373 J K

New Buildings

Sandhall Farm

B2095

F   G   H   **280**   J   K

Pannel
Farm

1

Carter's
Farm

2

Lunsford

**Pett
Level**

t Road

Chick Hill

Pett Level Road

Saxon Shore Way

Pett Road

3

Pett Road

Cliff End

Cliff End Lane

4

Saxon Shore Way

5

6

7

8

F   G   H   J   K

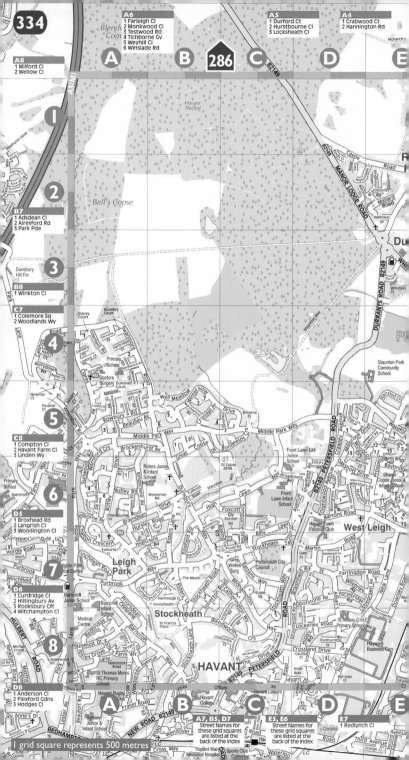

344

A B 296 C D E

1

2

3

Great Down

The Folly
▲ 112

Little Down

4

343

5

Courthill Farm

Butt Lane

Mill Lane

Dale Park

Baycombe Lane

6

Slindon College

Top Road

Church Hill

School Hill

Dyers Lane

Slindon

Park Lane

Beverlands Lane

Slindon Church of England School

B2132

Bridle Road

Sunnybox Lane

SHELLBRIDGE ROAD

Slindon Park

7

Slindon Wood N.T.

A29

Slindon Common N.T.

Mill Road

8

Hotel

Orchard Way

Fontwell Medical Centre

Fontwell

The Ridings

Arundel Road A27(T)

389

The Firs

West Wal...

Fontwell

A B C D E

F G H 297 J K

I

2

3

4

346

5

6

7

8

F G H 390 J K

Monarch's Way

B2139

Whiteways Lodge

A284 LONDON ROAD

A29

FAIRMILE BOTTOM A29

Madehurst

Parletts Farm

Cemetery

FAIRMILE BOTTOM

Fairmile Bottom

A29

Sherwood Rough

unchbowl

BN18

Rewell Wood

Rewell House

Long Lane

Long Lane

LONDON ROAD A284

LONDON

ROAD

A27(T) CHICHESTER ROAD Park Farm

Paine's Wood

Binsted Lane

CHICHESTER

ROAD

Elmer Lane

Canada

Ellis Close Hill Ter

Pearson Road

Arundel C of E Primary School

Oak End

Binsted Wood

Torton Hill

The Burgh

F G H **299** J K

I

2

3

Peppering
High Barn

Burpham
High Barn

Coombe Lane

Peppering Lane

4

348

Peppering
Farm

Hotel

PH

Burpham

5

Wepham

6

New
Down

7

W
We

Monarch's Way

8

Warningcamp

Blakehurst Lane

F G H **392** J K

Blakehurst

A   B   **300**   C   D   E

1

Welpham Down

Lee
Farm

2

Burpham
High Barn

3

Coombe Lane

4

Lower
Barpham

347

5

Upper
Barpham

6

New
Down

Monarch's Way

7

Welpham
Woods

Angmering
Park

8

Angmering
Park Farm

A   B   **393**   C   D   E

1 grid square represents 500 metres

F G H **301** J K

I

Cobden
Farm

2

Muntham

New
Barn

3

4

350

Tolmare Farm

5

Monarch's Way

Monarch's Way

Myrtle Grove
Farm

Monarch's Way

6

BN13

Longfurlong
Lane

7

Longfurlong
Barn

LONG FURLONG A280

LONG FURLONG A280

8

F G H **394** J K

Clapham
Wood

The Street

Patching

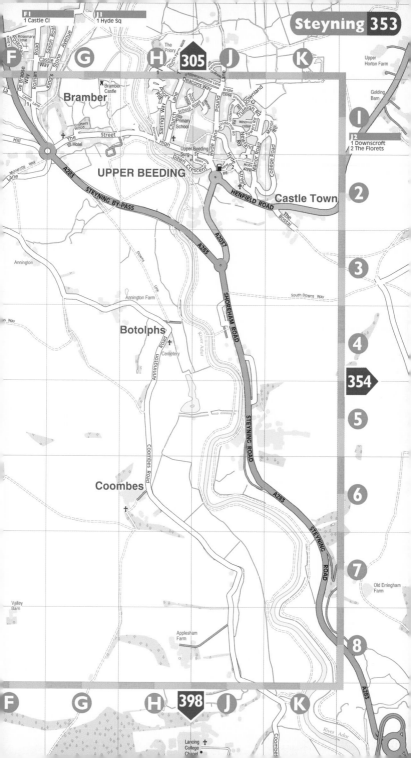

354

A B 306 C D E

Golding
Barn

1

College Road

2
Castle Town
The Bostall

3
South Downs Way

4

353

5

A283

6

STEYNING ROAD

7

8

Truleigh
Hill
213

Tottington
Barn

Freshcombe
Farm

The
Warren

Bu
Bo

Monarchs Way

Mill Hill

New Erringham
Farm

Old Erringham
Farm

BN43

A B 399 C D E
kingham
Barn

Slonk
Farm

River Adur

I grid square represents 500 metres

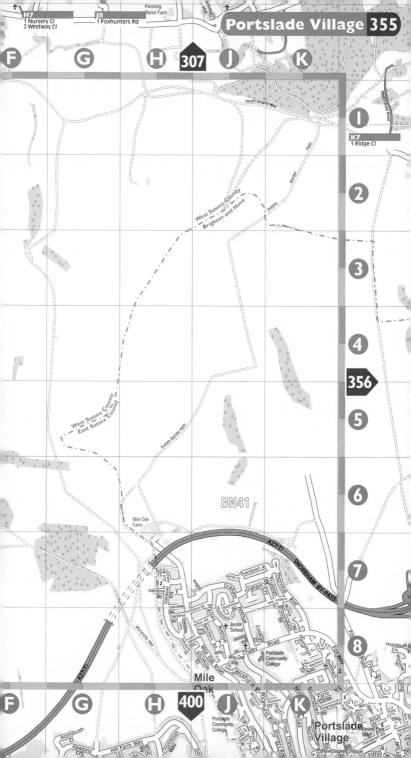

356

C8
1 The Dene

B8
1 Meads Cl
2 Meyners Cl
3 Sycamore Cl

Saddlescombe

A8
1 Juniper Cl
2 The Parks

A **B** **308** **C** **D** **E**

1

D8
1 Harmsworth Crs
2 Northease Dr
3 Northease Gdns

2

E8
1 Findon Cl
2 Midhurst Wk
3 Nutley Cl

South Downs Way

Devil's Dyke Road

Devil's Dyke Farm

Devil's Dyke Road

Brighton and Hove
West Sussex County

3

4

355

5

Skeleton Hovel

Mornington Way

Brighton & Hove
Golf Course

Devil's Dyke Road

6

A27(T)

SHOREHAM BY-PASS

7

A27(T)

Warren Road

Honey Croft

Buckley Cl

Hardwick Way

East Sussex
County Council

Hangleton Road

Hardwick Harmsworth

8

Portslade
Community
College

Benfield
Valley
Golf Course

Thornbush
Crs

Foredown Road

Meads Av

Helen's Crs

Pipers Cop

St Helen's Dr

Downsway

Sherbourne Road

Hangleton

Northease
Drive

Hangleton

**Portslade
Village**

A **B** **401** **C** **D** **E**

Fox Way

Dean Court Road

Hangleton La

Hangleton Way

Greenleas

Hangleton County
Junior & Infant

Sunningdale

Clcton
Avenue

Hangleton
Hove
Medical &
Welfare
Centre

Appleshaw

HANGLETON

Sunninghill

Fallowfield Crescent

Meadway Crescent

A2038

A29

I grid square represents 500 metres

314

A   B   C   D   E

Landport

South Malling

LEWES

Wallands Park

WESTERN ROAD

Southover

6   7

Iford

A   B   C   D   E

407

I grid square represents 500 metres

F G H **317** J K

I

Mark Cross

2

3

Lulhams Farm

Hall
Court Farm

4

366

Middle
Barn

Sheeplands
Farm

5

Bushy
Lodge Farm

LC

6

Middle
Farm

Pookhill
Barn

7

Sherrington
Manor

8

F G Charleston
Farmhouse H **410** J K

Tilton Farm

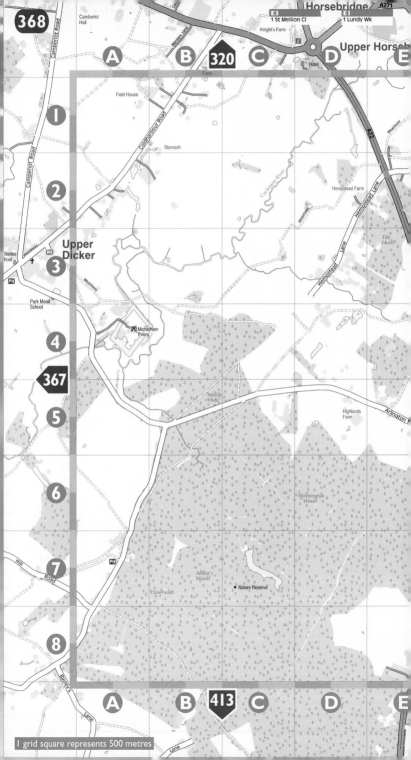

Down
370
AMBERSTONE
Under Road
Under Road
Lower Road

Amberstone
Grange Farm

BN27

322

Sac

(A)   (B)   (C)   (D)   (E)

(1) Gildridge Farm

Hurst Haven
Packeridge Stream

(2) Whelpley

(3) ashfoot Farm
New Bridge

Horse Eye Level

(4) Gemma Close

369
Lion House
Mill Road

(5) White Dyke Farm

Horse Eye

(6)

Slyes Farm
Downash

Pevensey Levels

(7)

Down Level

(8)

Glynleigh Level

(A)   (B)   (C)   (D)   (E)
Glyndle Manor

415

Rickney

I grid square represents 500 metres

F G H **323** J K

Golden Cross

Lower Road

Inn Stream

Cherry Croft
Farm

Church Road

Herstmonceux
Place

Herstmonceux Castle

Airy Road

Flamsteed
Road

Maskelyne Road

Church
Farm

Halley

1066 Country Walk

Road

Road

Graham Road

Wartling Road

I

Wartling Wood

Chame

The Well House

2

3

Cooper's Farm

Wartling

4

372

5

1066 Country Walk

Hurst Haven

Marsh Foot
Farm

6

7

Walk

Newhouse
Farm

Pylons Farm

8

F G H **416** J K

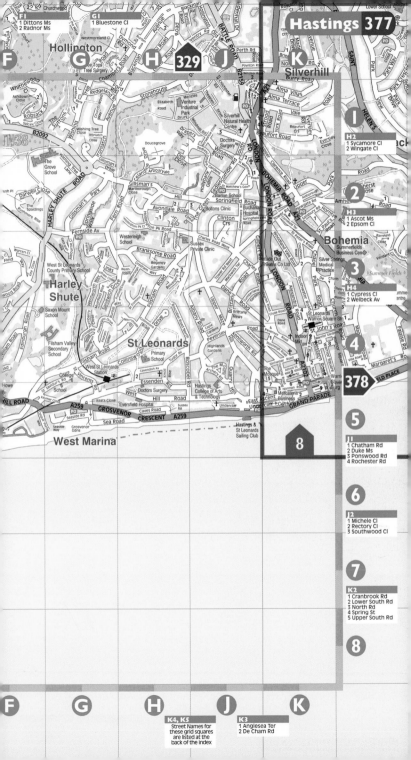

F1
1 Dittons Ms
2 Radnor Ms

G1
1 Bluestone Cl

Hollington

329

K
Silverhill

I

H2
1 Sycamore Cl
2 Wingate Cl

2

H3
1 Ascot Ms
2 Epsom Cl

Bohemia
Summerfields
Business Cen

3

H4
1 Cypress Cl
2 Welbeck Av

St Leonards

4

378

5

J1
1 Chatham Rd
2 Duke Ms
3 Ponswood Rd
4 Rochester Rd

8

West Marina

6

J2
1 Michele Cl
2 Rectory Cl
3 Southwood Cl

7

K2
1 Cranbrook Rd
2 Lower South Rd
3 North Rd
4 Spring St
5 Upper South Rd

8

F G H J K

K4, K5
Street Names for
these grid squares
are listed at the
back of the index

K3
1 Anglesea Ter
2 De Cham Rd

378

B2
1 Plitdown Cl

B3
1 Braybrooke Ter
2 Cornwallis Ter
3 Hillyglen Cl
4 Hopgarden Cl
5 Linton Crs
6 Station Ap

B4
1 Claremont
2 Dorset Pl
3 Prospect Pl
4 Robertson St
5 Schwerte Wy
6 White Rock Gdns

C1
1 Hughenden Pl

377

D2
1 Becket Cl
2 Gladstone Rd
3 Saunders Cl

D3
1 Alpine Rd
2 Castledown Av
3 Exmouth Pl
4 Gordon Rd
5 Swan Ter

E1
1 Broomgrove Rd
2 Robertsons Hl

B1
1 Hole Farm Cl

A3
1 De Cham Av
2 St Catherine's Cl
3 Summerfields

A2
1 Selmeston Cl

330

Broomsgrove

Blacklands

HASTINGS

West Hill

A4, C3, C4, D4
Street Names for
these grid squares
are listed at the
back of the index

E2
1 The Glebe

E3
Street Names for
these grid squares
are listed at the
back of the index

1 grid square represents 500 metres

F
1 High Bank Cl
2 Richmond St

1 Lodge Rd

Graystone
Lane

Alfred Road

Clive Vale

Belmont

All Saints
C Junior School

Doctors Surgery

Glenview
Close

Ecclesbourne Glen

Rocklands Lane

Saxon Shore Way

Nore

Fairlight Glen

Fairlight
Place

Barley Lane

Park

Covehurst

G1
1 Hawthorn Rd

F G H 331 J K

I
2
3
4
5
6
7
8

F G H J K

HAYLING ISLAND

I grid square represents 500 metres

384

E5
1 St Bart'lomews Cl

Oldwick Farm
West Stoke Road

C5
1 Appledram La (n)
2 St Chr'topher's Cl

C4
1 Frederick Rd

a Farm

Densworth

A Chalder Lane **B** **339** **C** **D** **E**

Sennicotts

B2178

West
Broyle House

West Stoke Road

1 Oakwood
Preparatory
School

OLD

BROYLE

Brandy

W Broyle
Way
Pine Grove

Salthill Road

ROAD

B2178

Northlands

2

Salthill
House

A27(T)

Salthill

Lane

Newlands

CHICHESTER

3 Poth

Clay Lane

Carleton
Gilb

Lane

Godwin
Way

4

Bethwines
Cl

Bethwines Farm

Mossie Gdns
Pollis Gdns

Blackboy Lane
Barker Rd
Newport Dr
Phillis Rd
Destino Av

Nursery

Bishop Luffa
C of E School

Paxman Avenue

Bishop Luffa
Oliver Whitby Rd
West Walberton Rd
Nevill Rd
Ashburnh

Parklands
County Primary
School

Beech C

LC

383

Fishbourne
Station

LC

Fishbourne
C of E
Primary School

Clay Lane

LC

West

Fishbourne

Bourne

Roman
Mews
Field

LC

Albert
Rd

Westmead
Rd

Westgate

Chiches
of A
& Te

MAIN

5 **ROAD**

A259

Beaver
Creek
Cl

FISHBOURNE ROAD
(WEST)

Mill La

Mill Cl

2

Fishbourne

Dolphin Ms

Road (East)

Clay Grove

LC

PO

FISHBOURNE ROAD (WEST)

1

CATHEDRAL
WAY

A259

Woodruf
Business

Philps
Bus Cen

6 Old
Park

Old Park Lane

A27(T)

CHICHESTER BY-P

Terr

7

8 k Farm

Lane

Appledram Lane (South)

†

Apuldram Lane (South)

Apuldram

BIRDHAM ROAD

A286

Gra

Corc
AV

Marden AV

A **B** **424** **C** **D** **E**

Dell Quay
Sailing Club

Dell
Bay

Hook Farm

Lane

Dell
Qua
Road

Mile End
Lane

Donningto
Manor

I grid square represents 500 metres

394

394

I

A **B** **349** **C** **D** **E**

Patching

Clapham

Clapham & Patching C of E Primary School

Selden Farm

Selden Lane

France Lane

The Street

Coldharbour Lane

Long Furlong

The Street

church cres

Selden

A280

2

Arundel Road

3

A27(T)

A27(T)

ARUNDEL ROAD

A280

WATER LANE

A280

Clapham Common

Ecc
lesden Farm

4

Woodlands

A2700

TITNORE LANE

393

A280

5

TITNORE LANE A2700

●Highdown Hill

6

Highdown Tower

Worthing Rugby Club ■

7

Hangleton

LITTLEHAMPTON ROAD

A259 A2032

8

Roundstone Farm

LITTLEHAMPTON ROAD

A259

Arlington Cresc

WORTHING ROAD

Saxon Close

Crossways

Russell's Close

North Lane

Somerset Road

Cissbury Close

Ferring Lane

Green Park

Greenview Avenue

Onslow Drive

Westergate Cl Easterga

Singleton Close

Singleton Crescent

BN

Gori
Sea

A **B** **434** **C** **D** **E**

EAST
PRESTON

Ferring Footba Club

St Andrews

St Oswald

FERRING

1 grid square represents 500 metres

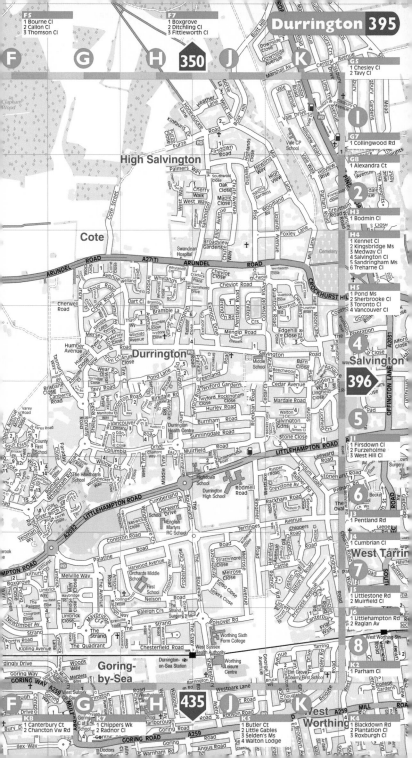

398

353

397

A5
1 Burley Cl
2 Fereday Cl
3 Mulberry Cl
4 North Farm Rd
5 Queensway
6 Robinson Cl

A4
1 Eighth Av
2 Glebe Cl
3 Grantsmead
4 Pemberton Cl

A3
1 Carisbrooke Cl

A6
1 Freshbrook Cl
2 Ingleside Rd
3 Meadow La
4 Rosecroft Cl
5 St Bernards Ct
6 The Tynings

A7
1 The Grovelands

B4
1 Mckerchar Cl

B5
1 Brierley Gdns

B6
1 Cowley Dr
2 The Saltings

C3
1 Old Shoreham Rd

E6
1 Wenceling Cots
2 Widewater Cl
3 Willow Cl

Lancing
College
Chapel

College Farm

North
Lancing

South
Lancing

Barn

BN15

I grid square represents 500 metres

406

Wildfowl
Reserve

A **B** **361** **C** **D** **E**

1

2

3

4

405

5

Brighton & Hove
East Sussex County

6

Balsdean
Farm

7

Pickers Hill Farm

8

Whiteway
Bottom

Brea
Botto

Coombe Farm

Brighton & Hove
East Sussex County

Upper Bannings Road

Homebush Av

Coombe Vale
Westfield Av
Westfield
Coombe
Coombe North
Vale Rd
Stanmer Av
Westfield Rise
Stanmer Av
Haldsean Av
Coombe Vale
Haldsean Rd
Coombe Rise

Whitcway Lane
Road
Farmer
Wivelsfield Road
Pickers Hill
Road
Perry Hill
Ridgewood
Avenue
Henstead Rd
Tumulus

Falmer
Avenue
Whiteston
Avenue
Luttrells
Lustrells
Close
Clinton
Crescent
Down
Close
Mount
Dr
Glynde
Av

Bishopstone Dr

A Saltdean County
School **B** **439** **C** **D** **E**

Rye
Close
Pedersburgh
Close

Saltdean

1 grid square represents 500 metres

Iford

F G H **362** J K

I

2

3

4

408

5

6

7

8

Northease
Manor
School

Northease Farm

White Way

Rodmell

The Dicklands

Badgers
Dene

The
Paddocks

Mill Lane

Rodmell
Primary School

Ilford Farm

LC

Southease
Station

Southease

Durham Farm

A26(T)

Dean's Farm

Money Burgh

Bullock Down

elscombe

The Lookout

Valley

Road

F G H **440** J K

Piddinghoe

Waterford
Close

Telscombe

St
Johns
Cl

Bretts
Field

Avenue

Heathdown
Close

Wendale
Drive

Highfield
Park

Greenacres

Halcombe Farm

F **G** Newelm **H** **364** ✝ **J** □ Firle Place **K**

Firle Bostal

I

Firle Plantation

2

South Downs way

Males Burgh

3

Blackcap Farm

Lord's Burghs

4

410

5

6

7

Five Bur

8

F **G** **H** **442** ▽ **J** **K**

Canteroose

Park Drive Close

Poverty Bottom

F8
1 Shepherds Cl

G7
1 Boship Cl
2 Broad Oak Cl
3 Caburn Cl
4 Chyngton Cl
5 Laughton Cl
6 Michelham Cl
7 Ringmer Wy

I7
1 Eskdale Cl
2 Hickling Cl
3 Horning Cl
4 Ranworth Cl
5 Reedham Rd
6 Whitbread Cl

H8
1 Lavender Cl

J6
1 Blatch'ton Mill Dr

J7
1 Borrowdale Cl
2 Buttermere Wy
3 Coniston Rd
4 Elmwood Cl
5 Elmwood Gdns
6 Middleham Wy
7 Wildwood

J8
1 Cleveland Cl
2 Harebell Cl
3 Magdalen Cl
4 Milfoil Dr
5 Sorrel Cl

K8
1 Marlborough Cl
2 Pentland Cl

Rickney

Glynleigh Road

Lusteds

Prieshawes

The Horns

Montague

Hankham CP School

Hankham

Foords Lane

Milton Street

Hankham Road

Peelings

Mill Hill

A27(T)

Peelings Lane

DITTONS ROAD

Stone Cross

Rattle Road

Mountney Level

Catsfield Cl

Rothorfield Avenue

Sorrel

Sorrel Drive

Pennine Way

Causeway Secondary School

Friday Street

Hide Hollow

B2191

Langney Shopping Cen

Langney

448

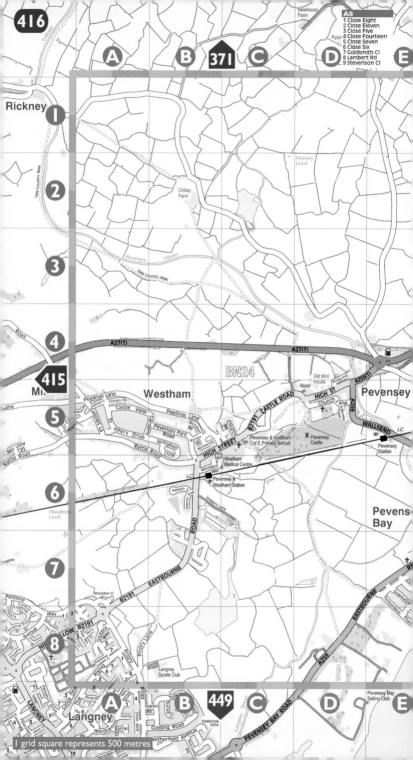

372

418

Middle Bridge

Walter's Haven

Old Haven

Rockhouse Bank

Norman's Bay Station

Coast Road

Mountney Dr

The Square

Arundel Close

The Boulevard

Haven

Marsfield Drive

Cam

South Close

Dove Close

Harold Close

Westham Drive

Westham Dr

Coast Road

Coast Road

Beachlands

Waverley Gdns

Coast Road

The Parade

SEA RD

The Promenade

Priory

Centre

Pevensey Bay

F G H J K

I 2 3 4 5 6 7 8

F G H J K

418

A B 373 C D E

1

Hooe
Level

2

Herbrand Walk

3

Rockhouse
Bank

Norman's Bay
Station

LC

Norman's
Bay

Coast Road

4

417

5

6

7

8

A B C D E

1 grid square represents 500 metres

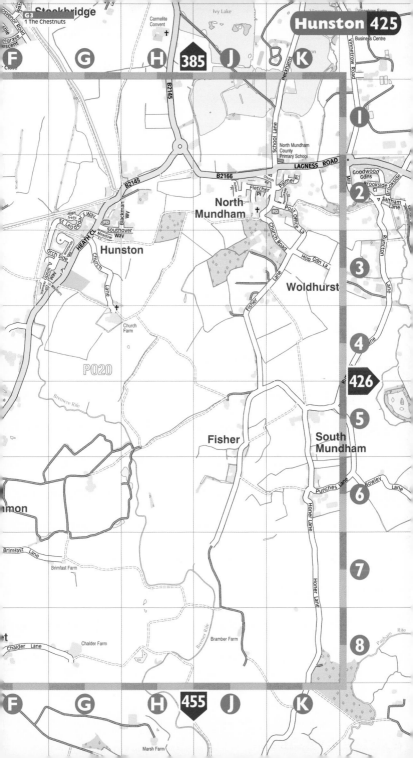

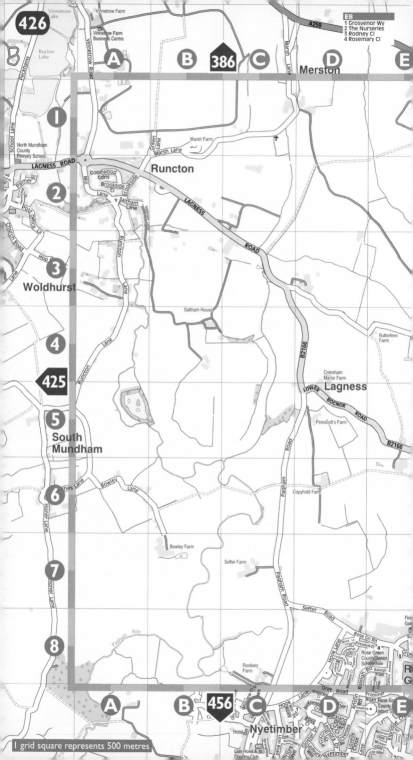

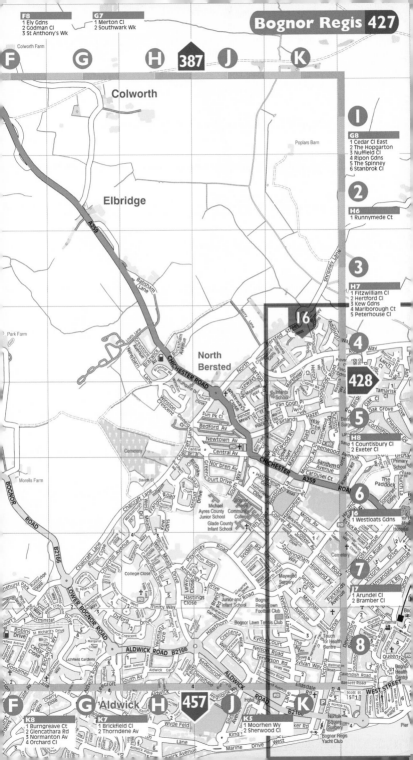

Yapton

430

St Marys
Meadow
Church
Briar Close
The Pines
Park Lee Rd
Loveys Road

A **B** nd **390** **C** **D** **E**

E3
1 Langmead Cl

B1
1 Wilson Ct

BURNDELL ROAD

Belmont
Park Rd
Park Dr
Fairholme

Fordwater
Gardens

Junction
Close

Beagle
Wick
Johnson
Way
Rollaston

Climping

Rudford
Industrial
Estate

Rudford
Industrial
Estate

1

Cherry Av
West
View

ROAD

2

BILSHAM
B2132

Bilsham

YAPTON

**Horsemere
Green**

Green Lane

Horsemere

ROAD

Apple
Tree
Walk

3

Grevatt's
Lane
West

GREVATT'S LANE

A259

CROOKTHORN LANE

CROOKTHORN

St M
Prim

Climping
Street

4

Ryebank Rife

Climping

429

Hotel

5

Middleton Business
Park

Ancton

Ancton
Lane

Elmer

Poole
Place

West
Av
First
Ancton Drive
Luckings
Crossway
Doctor
Surgery

Hedgehead
Kingsmead Pd
The Levns
Ancton
Lane
North Av
Elmer Dr
Arundel
Way
Elmer Cl
Poplar
Hard

Elmer Court

6

Middleton
Medical Centre

Southdean Dr
Shrubb
Drive
Thornton
Rose Av
West Central Drive
Freya Cl
The Jetty

Norfolk Way
Templesheen Rd
Sea
Manor
Wy

7

8

A **B** **C** **D** **E**

I grid square represents 500 metres

434

394
433

C3
1 April Cl
2 Chalet Cl
3 Ingle Green Cl

C2
1 Letchworth Cl

C1
1 Colindale Rd N
2 East Onslow Cl
3 Ferr'g C'ge Gdns
4 Greystoke Ms
5 The Grove

BN

Roundstone Farm

Arlington Cresc
OLD WORTHING ROAD
Saxon Close
Crossways

D2
1 Beehive Cl
2 Laburnum Cl

D3
1 Chalet Gdns
2 Doone End
3 Florida Gdns
4 Guernsey Rd
5 Lamorna Gdns
6 Milbury Cl

E1
1 Thakeham Cl

EAST PRESTON

West Kingston

East Kingston

Meadow Park

Kingston Lane

Sea Lane

Peak Lane

Middle Way

Gorse Avenue

stal Road

Onslow Drive

St Andrews Way

Ferring Football Club

FERRING

Primary School

Goring

Goring Way

Thakeham Drive

Midhurst Drive

Singleton Crescent

Elm Pk

Sea Lane Gdns

Beehive Lane

Somerset Road

Ferringham Way

West Drive

Ferring Marine

South Drive

Sea Drive

Marine

The Strand

1 grid square represents 500 metres

436

396

435

WORTHING

12

13

A **B** **C** **D** **E**

1 Highgrove Gdns

A1
1 Dorchester Gdns
2 Lansdowne Ct
3 The Rowans
4 West Av

B2
1 Boundary Cl

C1
1 Elizabeth Rd
2 Park Crs
3 Richmond Ct
4 Treveor Cl

C2
1 Brunswick Rd
2 Milton St
3 Western Rw

D1
1 Chapel Rd
2 Grafton Pl
3 Grosvenor Rd
4 Humphrys Rd
5 Stoke Abbott Rd

D2
1 Montague Pl
2 New St
3 Prospect Pl

E1
1 Alfred Pl
2 Warwick Pl

1 grid square represents 500 metres

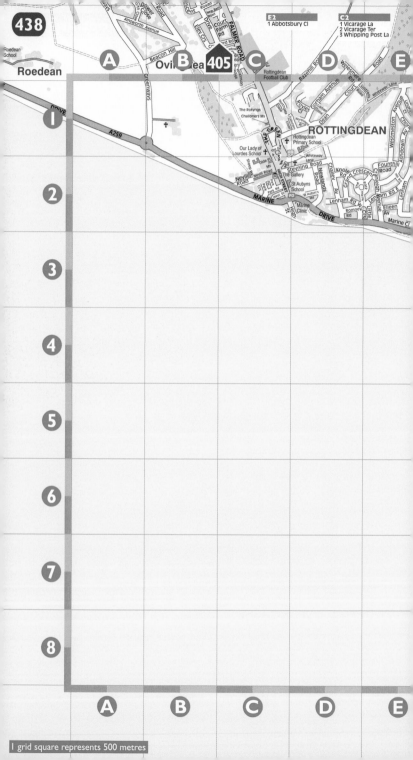

K2
1 Berry Cl
2 Chatsworth Av
3 Northcote La
4 Park View Cl
5 St Laurence Cl
6 Tye Vw

K3
1 Park View Ri

Coombe Farm

Coombe Vale

Westfield Av

Coombe Rise

F   G   H   406   J   K

Brighton & Hove
East Sussex County

Saltdean

Pedlersburgh

K4
1 Lincoln Av South
2 Second Rd
3 Third Rd

I

Saltdean County School

Doctors Surgery

Telscombe Cliffs

Telscombe Cliffs Primary School

A259 SOUTH COAST ROAD

Hoddern County Junior School

SOUTH COAST ROAD

A259

St Peter's Av

The Esplanade
The Esplanade
Doctors Surgery

S COAST RD   A259

440

Doctors Surgery

2

3

4

5

6

7

8

F   G   H   J   K

Newhaven 441

G1
1 Cedarwell Cl
2 Shepherds Cl

G3
1 Piddinghoe Mead

F **G** **H** 408 **J** **K**

South Heighton

1

G4
1 Hawthorn Ri
2 Hazel Cl
3 Lapierre Rd
4 Lewry Cl

2

H3
1 Ship St

3

H4
1 Cloisters
2 Jackson Ms
3 Lower Pl
4 Murray Av
5 Neill's Cl
6 Newfield La
7 Newfield Rd

4

NEWHAVEN

442

5

H5
1 Northdown Cl

6

I1
1 Glynde Cl
2 Iford Cl
3 Tarring Cl

7

J2
1 Cottage Cl
2 St Martins Crs

8

J4
1 Bay Vue Rd
2 Bridge St
3 Chapel St
4 Dacre Rd
5 Hill Side
6 Lorraine Rd
7 Senlac Rd
8 South La
9 South Wy

18 19

Harbour Heights

F **G** **H** **J** **K**

K3
1 Estate Rd

K2
1 Powell Gdns

K1
1 Rookery Cl
2 Vicarage Cl

East Blatchington

Sutton

EASTBOURNE

BN25

410

444

458

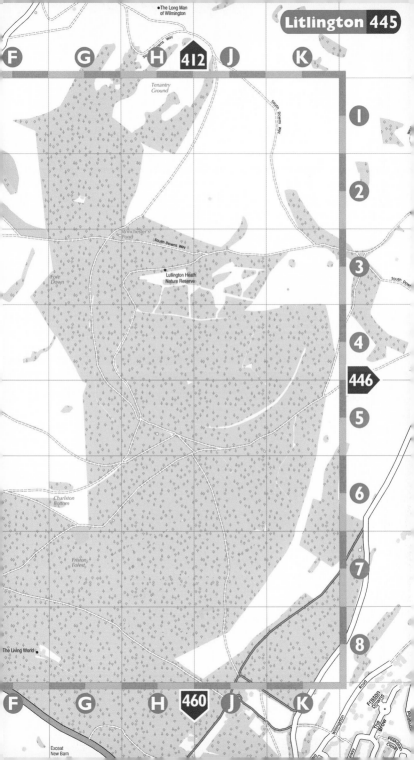

The Long Man
of Wilmington

F   G   H   **412**   J   K

I

2

South Downs Way

Tenantry
Ground

Winchester's
Pond

South Downs Way

3

South Down

Fore
Down

Lullington Heath
Nature Reserve

4

446

5

6

Charlston
Bottom

7

Friston
Forest

8

The Living World

F   G   H   **460**   J   K

Friston Forest

Wilmington

The Brow

Exceat
New Barn

Peakdean Close

G1
1 Cleevelands
2 Willingdon Wy

G2
1 Hoo Gdns
2 Willingdon Cl

G6
1 Lennox Cl
2 Maxfield Cl
3 Victoria Rd

G7
1 The Sanctuary

H1
1 Canterbury Cl

H2
1 Shortlands Cl

H3
1 Warburton Cl

H4
1 Chalvington Rd
2 Jack O'dandy Cl

H5
1 Gresham Cl
2 Newick Rd
3 Willingdon Rd

H7
1 Victoria Gdns

H8
1 Ridge Lands Cl

I6
1 Yielding's Cl

K7
1 New Up'rton Rd
2 The Quadrant
3 Selwyn Dr
4 Torfield Rd

K1
1 Blackthorn Cl
2 Petworth Pl
3 Thornwood Cl

Willingdon

Hampden Park

EASTBOURNE

Downside

Old Town

Upperzon

BN22

BN21

F1
1 Close Eighteen
2 Close Fifteen
3 Close Four
4 Close Ten
5 Close Twelve
6 Close Twentyfour
7 Spring Lodge Cl

F2
1 Chailey Cl
2 Redford Cl
3 Slindon Crs

F3
1 Ethelred Cl
2 Fair Isle Cl

F4
1 Cochrane Cl
2 Foley Cl
3 Gardner Cl
4 Middleton Dr
5 Somerville Cl
6 Vernon Cl
7 Woodward Cl

F5
1 Cook Av
2 Nelson Dr
3 Palliser Cl

G4
1 Ayscue Cl
2 Boscawen Cl
3 Cornwallis Cl
4 Rodney Cl
5 Vincent Cl

G5
1 Pound Cl
2 Royal Sov'ign Vw

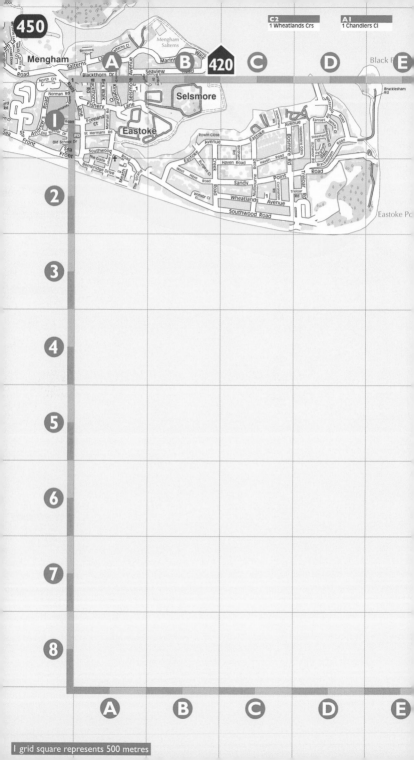

I grid square represents 500 metres

F **G** **H** 423 **J** **K**

Holt Place
B2179
Pinks Lane
Mapsons

Hillands Farm

Batchmere Road
First Avenue
I

Hundredsteine Ln
BELL LANE

Somerley
Carthagena Farm
Somerley Lane
Batchmere's Farm

Tile Barn Lane
Second Avenue
2

B2198
Mill House

Stubcroft Lane
Bookers Lane

Third Avenue
Avenue Lane
3

bcroft Farm
Almodington

Almodington Lane

Clayton Lane
Earnley Road
4

Holden's Farm
Earnley Grange

BRACKLESHAM LANE
454 ...on Farm
Earnley Mnr Close
Barton Av
Clappers Lane

n Close
Graywood Av
Elm Close
Earnley
5

eech Av
Drove Lane

Harmony Dr
El Conlia Lane
Manston
Avebury
Bracklesham
6

Malmsley Av
Third
Sussex Gv
Marsh Farm
Brackesham Road
Seafield Drive
Shell Vw

Stoney Lane
7

Sussex Beach Holiday Village

Broad Rife
8

F **G** **H** **J** **K**

Bracklesham Bay

454

A B 424 C D E

Mapsons Lane

Hillands
Farm

Highleigh Road

Lockgate Road

Fletchers

Rotten Row

STREET END ROAD

Burnham Lane

Fletchers Lane

1 Batchmere's Farm

Batchmere Road

First Avenue

Highleigh

2 Second Avenue

Critchel's Lane

Green Lane

3 Almodington

Almodington Avenue

Keynor House

Sidlesham
County
Primary
School

Ke

Glebecute Lane

4

453

Easton Farm

Ham Lane

Cow Lane

Chalk Lane

Easton Lane

5

The Elms

Bakers F

6

Oakhurst Farm

7

Greenwood Farm

Porthole
Farm

8

Broad Rife

Ham Farm

A B 464 C D E

Selsey
Country Club

1 grid square represents 500 metres

F   Chalder Lane   Chalder Farm   G   H   **425**   J   K

I

Marsh Farm

Honer Farm

2

Rookery Lane

Rookery Farm

Halsey's Farm

Church Lane   3   **Pagham**

Mahwood Lane

Mill Lane

PH

4

Wood Lane

456

Pagham Lagoon

Pagham Harbour
(Nature Reserve)

5

Pagham Harbour

Ferry House

6

B2145

7

Home Farm   Church Norton

Norton   8

Coles Farm

Greenlease Farm

F   G   Rectory Lane   Grange Lane   H   **465**   J   K

Grange Farm

456

456

D1
1 Avian Gdns

C3
1 Channel Vw

C2
1 Canterbury Cl
2 Hadlands

A B **426** C D E

G

1

D2
1 Malvern Wy

Nyetimber

Hotel

Lion Hotel &
Country Club

Sylvia Cl
Summer Lane

Pagham
Cricket Club

Football Club

Horns
Lane

Barton Cl

Church

Sussex Drive

2

E1
1 Cottage Cl
2 Stoney Stile Cl
3 Valentines Gdns

Abbotsbury

Payne

West
Drive

Manor Way

3

E2
1 Hunters Cl
2 The Orchard
3 Singleton Cl
4 Sudbury Cl

Pagham

Church Lane

Pagham Road

Queensmead

St Thomas Dr

The Cswy

Arun
Way

The Fairway

Viscount
Drive

4

Heron
Md

Swan Dene

Wyrthering
Cl

Sea
Lane

West Road

Griffiths
Clinic

Pagham
Yacht
Club

455

Lagoon

Harbour
Road

West Front Road

5

Pagham
Lagoon

6

7

8

A B C D E

I grid square represents 500 metres

F1
1 Alborough Wy
2 Grangewood Dr
3 Hamilton Gdns
4 Old Farm Cl
5 Tangmere Gdns

F2
1 Coastguard Pde
2 Fisherman's Wk
3 Seacourt Cl

G1
1 Ch'kmare C'pice
2 Cheveley Gdns
3 Edinburgh Cl
4 Little Babbsham
5 Ludlow Cl
6 Redwood Pl
7 Stanmore Gdns

G2
1 Aldwick Hundred
2 Strange Gdn

H1
1 Mauldmare Cl
2 Raycroft Cl
3 Shipfield
4 Thrusloes
5 Wallfield
6 Woodstock Gdns

J1
1 Wessex Av

K1
1 Charlwood St
2 Oxford St
3 Park Ter
4 St Winifred's Cl
5 Swansea Gdns
6 Victoria Rd South
7 Wood St

SEAFORD

C1
1 Sunningdale Cl

B1
1 Bramber Cl
2 Steyne Cl

A1
1 Chatham Pl
2 Church La
3 Mallett Cl
4 Pelham Yd
5 West St

E1
1 Fairways Cl
2 Mark Cl
3 Newick Cl
4 Poynings Cl
5 Steyning Cl

Seaford Station

Golf Course

Hill Fort

Seaford Head

I grid square represents 500 metres

The Living World

NE | ROAD
PH
Exceat Bridge
A359

F **G** **H** **444** **J** **K**

Cuckmere River

South Downs Way

Vanguard Way

Seven Sisters Country Park

Foxhole

South Downs Way

Nature Reserve

Cuckmere Haven

Cliff End

Vanguard Way

South Downs Way

Seven Sisters

460 South Dov

I
2
3
4
5
6
7
8

F **G** **H** **J** **K**

F2
1 Downlands Wy
2 Lindon Cl

F3
1 Wayside

F

G

H

446

J

K

Pea Down

Ringwood

Friston Downs

The Brow

Peakdean Lane

Peakdean Close

Dene

Michel Close

The Link

High Close

Summerdown Lane

Road

Dene Close

Elven La

Downsview Lane

Doctors Surgery

Michel

Hillside

Side

Dene

Cottages Gdns

Venn Close

A259

Eastdean Down

East Dean

BN20

Gilberts Drive

Street

Gap Road

Birling Farm

Cornish Farm

Crapham Down

Long Down

Beachy Head Road

Hodcombe Farm

South Downs Way

I

Eastbou... Golf Clu... Ho...

G2
1 Elven La
2 Michel Dene Cl
3 Went La

A259

2

B2103

WARREN

EAST DEAN ROAD

3

4

462

5

Bullock Down

6

7

8

F

G

H

J

K

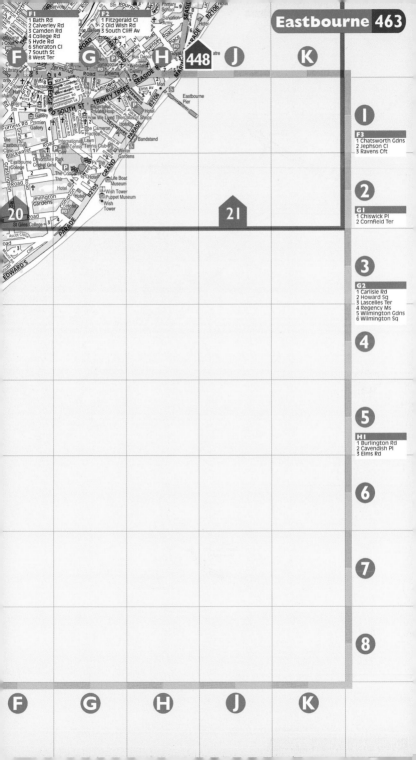

F1
1 Bath Rd
2 Calverley Rd
3 Camden Rd
4 College Rd
5 Hyde Rd
6 Sheraton Cl
7 South St
8 West Ter

F2
1 Fitzgerald Cl
2 Old Wish Rd
3 South Cliff Av

F3
1 Chatsworth Gdns
2 Jephson Cl
3 Ravens Cft

G1
1 Chiswick Pl
2 Cornfield Ter

G2
1 Carlisle Rd
2 Howard Sq
3 Lascelles Ter
4 Regency Ms
5 Wilmington Gdns
6 Wilmington Sq

H1
1 Burlington Rd
2 Cavendish Pl
3 Elms Rd

E4
1 Grant Cl

D3
1 Broadway

C3
1 Cross Eels
2 Mayridge

454

E5
1 Ursula Av North

E6
1 Beaufield Cl

Selsey
Country Club

Duck La
Chainbridge
Marigold

Teal Lane

Peter's Cl

Lobster
Prawn Cl

Mackerel La

Warner's Lane
Spinney

Freeways

Montalan Crs
The Wadeway

Coppice La
Old McNair
Cordwainers Rd
Paddock

Selsey
Cricket

Mill Lane

Drift Lane
Caravans

Indoor
Tadds Cott
Gallery

West Sands
Leisure Centre

The Horse
Knob

School

Comm
Colleg

Hersee Way

Thorney Dr

West Street

Coxes Rd
Murray Rd
Bonnar Cl
Bonnar Road

Latham

HILLFIELD ROAD B2145

Vincent Rd

Warner Road
Carton Rd
Sea Gr

Peachey Road
The Bridgeway
Seal

Gree

Danefield Road

Marine
Gdns
Seal

Norton

F · G · H · **455** · J · K

Coles Farm

Greenlease Farm

Grange Lane

Grange Farm

1

Links Lane

Park Farm

Park Lane

East Beach

Inner Owers

2

St George's Close

Manor Farm

The Willows

Church Road

Mountwood Road

3

Wellington Rd

Denny's Close

Glen House Cl

County ary ool

North Wy

Orpen Pl

Landseer

Gainsborough

Lindfield Way

Broad View

4

Manor Rd

Cottage

Sunny

Albion Road

5

James Street

SELSEY

Jones Sq

Lifeboat Wy

Sparshott Rd

Wight Wy

Pennycord

6

Selsey Bill

7

8

F · G · H · J · K